STAND YOUR
GROUND

Standing Firm in the Face of Adversity

ROBERT NULL

ISBN 979-8-88644-387-5 (Paperback)
ISBN 979-8-88644-388-2 (Digital)

Covenant Books
11661 Hwy 707
Murrells Inlet, SC 29576
www.covenantbooks.com

Pastoral ministry is rewarding, rigorous, fulfilling, and frustrating. In this book, *Stand Your Ground*, Pastor Bob Null draws attention to the leadership lessons seen in the life of David. David's path from the pasture to the palace was marked by highs and lows, victories and defeats, gains and losses. And so goes the pastorate. The ministry journey of a pastor is also marked by highs and lows, those who befriend you, and those who betray you. How a pastor responds to all that goes with loving, leading, comforting, and correcting God's people will determine much of that pastor's effectiveness and happiness in ministry. This book is insightful, impactful, and inspirational. *Stand Your Ground* is a must-read for every pastor.

—Bob Wilburn
Superintendent Mississippi District Assemblies of God

Pastor Bob has written from his heart to those called by God to be a pastor or leader in a congregation. I believe that every person in ministry and every person considering ministry as a vocation should read this book. You may be called and anointed of God to lead a congregation that has no clue how to follow a biblical pastor. Through this book, we are pointed to men in the Bible that were called and anointed to serve but found themselves with difficulties that they never dreamed possible. Their "but God" moments become clear examples for us when they decided to stand their ground. The book offers a realistic look at the life and role of a pastor *standing his ground.*

—Edgar L. Reed
Global Director of Projects
Life Publishers International
Assemblies of God Missionary

Stand Your Ground is the kind of book that takes a lifetime of experience to write. I highly recommend it. Inside you will find heartache and encouragement sitting side by side.

This book does a great job of taking ancient biblical events and applying relevancy to today. You're going to want to have a notebook nearby while you are reading it. Not only will this book give you biblical insights that can be used every day, but it will also inspire you. After reading this book you will be convinced that no matter how difficult, the goal is attainable. Step into God's will and stand your ground.

—Mickey Smith
Author, Lay Leader, Deacon

CONTENTS

INTRODUCTION

But recall the former days in which, after you were illuminated, you endured a great struggle with sufferings: partly while you were made a spectacle both by reproaches and tribulations, and partly while you became companions of those who were so treated; for you had compassion on me in my chains, and joyfully accepted the plundering of your goods, knowing that you have a better and an enduring possession for yourselves in heaven. Therefore do not cast away your confidence, which has great reward. For you have need of endurance, so that after you have done the will of God, you may receive the promise.
—Hebrews 10:32–36 (NKJV)

They were rugged, daring, and courageous. They could be counted on when things got tense. These men regularly engaged in great exploits on behalf of their king. They defeated their enemies, led Israel to victory, and helped David, the son of Jesse, establish a nation. These men stood as amazing role models for others to follow and remain as relevant today as ever. Their examples of tenacity and bravery set the standard for men and women of God through the ages. We should be inspired by their courage, compelled by their commitment, and as consumed with our cause as they were to theirs. We should note that 2 Samuel 23 is not where any of these men began. They became King David's mighty men of valor. They stood through trials in their earlier days that helped them to develop into the men we celebrate and admire when we read the pages of Scripture.

This book is about standing firm in the face of adversity. I think the willingness to stand is not something that we learn to do but rather that we are inspired to do. When we stand, we give the Lord something to work with. We give him someone to anoint for a purpose, someone to use for his cause. The willingness to stand arises from having seen others do so or having been inspired through his word. Standing firm in the face of adversity is also a matter of character. Pastors, people, and churches often find themselves with the choice of standing firm or fleeing. Those who stand are guaranteed a fight. Those who flee are guaranteed a failure. Since this is the case, standing, looking for God's victory, seems to be the proper course.

Satan's snares, the lure of sin, faulty character traits, and dumb mistakes can bring individuals and churches to their knees. The one-hundred-year-old church that I pastor had experienced generations of leadership struggles, power plays, and outward antagonism from long-term board members toward former pastors. Bad leadership habits among the pastoral staff and deacons of days gone by had taken the church off course. Eventually, sin took hold of those in leadership and left ruin and destruction in its wake. In spite of this being true, not only did the church survive, it thrives. In many ways, this church could stand as an example today for others to follow: passionately in love with Jesus, genuinely loving one another, and chasing the vision that God has set before us. We are pressing toward the goal.

We have not arrived. Far from it! There will always the occasional feathers to be unruffled. Unexpected staff changes require significant adjustment. Maintenance issues with older buildings frequently crop up. More financial strength would always be helpful. What I am describing is a church that has walked through the fire and the flood and is still on its feet. This is a body that has learned to keep its collective eyes on Jesus and remember the call. When you know that you are standing in the place of God's choosing, it is worth the fight. Still, you must be courageous, committed, and consumed by the cause.

There are many churches that have similar experience. Tons of churches are of equal age and have encountered equivalent problems along the way. Troubles arise for us all. People are people. The difference here is that, as a church, we have learned the lessons of unity not only with each other but in vision. Hebrews 10:32–36 serves as a perfect story line of a people who flourish despite opposition and stand beside others during their struggles. The endurance of stout-hearted believers serves as an example for others.

When we consider the heroes of Scripture like King David and his mighty men, we must know that they all felt the pain of rejection as well as the thrill of victory. Each one experienced the nervousness of the coming battle, felt the weariness of the campaign, and maybe even the fear of defeat. Yet they kept going. Surely their emotions were much like ours. There were times that they suffered deep disappointment, as have we all. Every one of us has suffered the discouragement of having been deserted on the field of battle. Those of us who stay in the fight have also felt the thrill of accomplishment in the Lord. We have embraced the joy of seeing the vision come to pass and have tasted victory over the schemes of our adversary. The chapters of this book all begin with an imaginative "what-if" before entrance into the subject of the chapter. What did the heroes of the Bible feel that the scripture is silent about? What may have been their underlying stories? Bear with me as I fill in the blanks of these stories with plausible "what-ifs." I hope you enjoy their examples and the words of these pages as we *stand our ground.*

CHAPTER 1

REMEMBER

Sometimes the Lord gives us what we want even when it is not really what we need. That was the case for Israel. The leaders of the people had begun to insist that Israel be ruled by a king like the surrounding nations. So when the Lord pointed out that he had chosen Saul, the son of Kish, from the tribe of Benjamin, the old prophet did not hesitate. Samuel took him aside, shared with him what the Lord was doing, and anointed him to become king over Israel. A few days later, Samuel gathered the leaders of the tribes of Israel together, introduced their king, and instructed them in the manner of royalty. He had faithfully followed the direction of the Lord and strongly admonished Israel that they were expected to *"fear the Lord and serve him in truth with all of their hearts."* As Samuel instructed the people, they began to realize that their actions were a rejection of the Lord and his leadership in their lives. But it was too late.

In no time, the new king blew it. He demonstrated himself to be impatient, impulsive, unfaithful, and dishonest. He usurped the priestly role of Samuel and ignored the direction of the Lord on more than one occasion. When Saul was confronted by Samuel, he denied and lied. "It was the people's fault, not mine." Samuel's attempted correction and instruction fell on deaf ears as Saul simply did what he wanted. Finally, the Lord told Samuel that he was rejecting Saul as king, and they would need an eventual replacement.

The Lord directed Samuel to go to Bethlehem, to a man named Jesse, and anoint one of his sons to become king. One by one, the sons came before the prophet. One by one, they were rejected by the Lord until they came to the youngest son, David, who had been keeping the sheep. As soon as Samuel saw David, the Lord said, *"Arise and anoint this one!"* From that day forward, the spirit of the Lord rested upon David. At the same time, the spirit of the Lord was lifted from King Saul.

In the spring, Israel and the Philistines had gathered their armies for battle in the Valley of Elah. Though the armies were gathered, forty days passed without fighting. Every day, a giant from the Philistine camp stepped forward and issued a challenge. He would insult the Israelites and their God and challenge them to send out a champion to face him. In response, they would walk away. Old Jesse knew that his elder sons were gathered with the army of Saul and sent David with supplies for his brothers. David arrived in the camp with his cargo of grain, bread, and cheese just in time to hear the challenge from Goliath. He also saw his brothers and the other men of Israel slip away in fear.

Whether it was the brashness of youth or the spirit of the Lord, we may never know. But David was offended and angered at the giant's words. His anger turned to action, and David went out to face the giant. What a sight it must have been for a child of fifteen or so, standing before a nine-foot giant. Yet when the dust had settled, the giant was dead, and David had only thrown one rock. Israel rallied and defeated the Philistine army, and young David had become the hero of the day. Sometimes you must remember who you are and do what's right.

Remember

> But recall the former days in which, after you were illuminated, you endured a great struggle with sufferings. (Hebrews 10:32 NKJV)

Remember those early days after you received the light (Hebrews 10:32). Do you remember when your faith was new and fresh? Remember when you were newly born again? Remember the early days after you received the light? Remember the promises that he has made to you? Think of the freshness that you felt when you first committed your life to Jesus. You were suddenly washed clean from your sin. An unexplained joy surged into your life, and you felt his strength. You had a new bounce in your step, a new strength in your soul, and a new focus for your life. There was as much a realization of your need for God as there was a newfound access to him. You felt a kinship with other Christians that you had never before known. The purpose of your life began to be defined. You had become a new creation; the old things of your life were washing away. Do you remember the realization of your call into the ministry or the first inkling of your purpose in his kingdom? Of course, you do! That is why you are here. You may very well be the Shammah of your generation. You may be the one sent to remind others of the purpose and plan of God for their lives. You might be the champion of the moment.

Your main purpose may be to stir your own and others' memories. Remember how and where you have stood. In addition, remember with whom you have stood!

Every believer has encountered resistance and outright attack. Our adversary is well practiced and persistent. He is determined to keep you from the Father's best by any means possible. His roaring, his arrows, and his accusations are damaging if they find their mark. But remember, even though resistance is frustrating and hurtful, it is not defeat. Arrows shot are not wounds, and roaring is not truth. The enemy is really nothing more than a loud noise and a great distraction. That's only when you allow him to be. He may be out to *steal, kill, and destroy*, but *greater is he that is in you than he that is in the world. Remember it!* Another thing to remember is that not every difficulty is the devil! Sometimes life just gets messy. *A good persistent memory is essential to living a successful Christian life.*

Remembering who you are in Jesus is vital. Practice in your heart the identity he has given you. *"I am a child of the King." "Greater it he that is in me... I am the righteousness of God in Christ Jesus... I am*

3

more than a conqueror through him who loves me... I know the plans that I have for you says the Lord..." The promises of God are yes and amen in Christ Jesus, and we overcome by *the blood of the lamb and the word of our testimony.* Our testimonies begin with salvation and include those things we have received from God the Father, experienced in our lives, and have persistently held in our memories. Yet they do not become testimonies until we rehearse them in our own minds and begin to share them with other believers. This sharing creates an investment of faith in the author of our faith. It keeps God's success in our lives at the forefront of our minds and reminds us to *look unto the hills where our help comes from.* And finally, the sharing of our testimony creates an atmosphere of encouragement and accountability that enables us to be a source of strength for others. Galatians 6 reminds us to *bear one another's burdens and so fulfill the law of Christ.* At times, the burdens of others are borne upon the words of our testimonies. For it is through these testimonies that people are inspired to believe that God will help them in their times of need.

Never forget your beginnings

It is important to remember where you started. *Remember the early days after you received the light!* When you were first saved, you viewed everything with wonder. The Word was fresh. Your life seemed fresh. You were innocent in your faith. Your enthusiasm for the things of God was unimpeded. You were successful in serving because you had received the light of God into your life. There seemed to be not only fresh grace but extra grace! He had made you into a brand-new creation. Your potential and promise were at their apex, and you could dream. However, today, if you have been saved for a while, you will likely have to persist or persevere to dream the dreams of faith.

The dreams of our faith are central to persevering. We must see where we are going with God! *Without a vision, the people perish...* If Satan can subdue the saints to the point of dreamless existence, he has won. A child of God who cannot see beyond today has a sure

4

end in sight. It is vision that encourages us to grow, to stretch, and to strive. Vision shows us what can be. It is important to develop the ability to see things as they will be rather than stay focused on the way things are. If we have no dreams, we will have little hope. Little hope means no real faith. Interestingly enough, this forward-looking hope, clarity of purpose, and plan of God for your life called vision is kindled by and related to an understanding of where you began in Christ. If you know where you have been, you should have little problem seeing where you are going.

Hebrews 11 says, "*Now faith is the substance of things hoped for and the evidence of things not yet seen.*" In this passage, *substance* literally means the "realization of," and *evidence* implies "confidence." Clearly, faith and hope are closely related to one another and necessary for the realization of the promises of God. It is imperative that we be able to hope, to dream, and to expect that God will do what he says He will do. Even our salvation is tied to this kind of hope. Romans 8:24–25 says, "*For we are saved in this hope, but hope that is seen is not hope...but if we hope for what we do not see, then we eagerly wait for it with perseverance.*" If we truly have faith and hope in the promises of God, we will be able to dream the dreams of faith that will grant us vision for those things to come. That vision will remain regardless of the difficulties or delays that we encounter along the way. *We eagerly wait with perseverance.*

I once had a pastor who said, "If I had one hundred new Christians in my church, I believe we could put the fires of hell out!" What he was saying was, new believers believe. They are fresh and unfrazzled. They live so close to the change that took place in their lives they believe God can change anything. They are in love with God, love their churches, and love the opportunity to be used by God. They are so close to the beginning they have no trouble remembering.

The problem with many people is that they store everything in their memory the same way and have not discriminated between good and bad, God and man, kind of memories. Many men and women of God develop jaded attitudes. They feel they can predict outcome based on past disappointments. There is nothing wrong with being wise and watching for attacks, roadblocks, and potholes in the road of faith. However, we cannot afford to develop a pessimistic point of view. If we do, it will not be long before we are surrounded by an army of pessimists.

A spirit-filled servant of God (ministry or layman) should be optimistic and full of hope. He is on the winning team. Hope should be alive in his heart. Our God is able. *"Now to Him who is able to do exceedingly abundantly above all that we ask or think"* (Ephesians 3:20 NKJV). Pessimistic Christian is a contradiction in terms. It is also a clear indication of memory problems. If you forget what he did for you, it will be difficult for you to expect him to do anything for others. The result of "Christian pessimism" is a nation of churches stuck in maintenance mode just waiting for the rapture. They have no outreach and very little victory, just a gathering of people looking for relief.

We need a resurgence of remembrance! Our people and our pastors need to regain the sense of freshness and wonder that came with the new birth. The revelation of John says, *"They overcame him by the blood of the lamb and the word of their testimony."* It is the remembering of God's grace that enables our testimonies to be rehearsed. Rehearsing our testimonies stimulates our faith, and in turn, we develop fresh testimonies.

CHAPTER 2

STAND YOUR GROUND

King Saul had forgotten his beginnings. When he was first chosen to be king, he was humbled and a bit embarrassed. In fact, when the prophet Samuel called him forward, they found him hiding. He had never imagined that he would find himself in such a position. Yet here he is, chosen by God and anointed by the prophet Samuel as the first king of Israel. The trouble is, it turns out that obedience is harder than imagined. Saul had been scolded more than once by the prophet, and the last time, Samuel even said that he had lost the kingdom. How could that be? He was still the king. He decided that he would stand his ground even if it meant doing the wrong thing.

Saul began to feel paranoid. He had to keep an eye on potential competitors. So far, a young man named David was the only one who appeared to raise cause for concern. By some fluke, David had killed the giant, Goliath, and everybody instantly loved him. Sure, he volunteered when no one else would. The boy seemed to have an unnatural confidence. He had killed the giant when no one else would step up. After Goliath, David defeated every enemy that Saul sent him against. The men of war admired him, and the young ladies sang songs celebrating David's heroics. Yet he was humble. To make matters worse, there were rumors that Samuel had secretly anointed David to become the next king.

How? What? Who does he think he is? There is already a king in Israel! If Saul has anything to say about it, that youngster will never become king. Saul had become good at getting rid of threats. Well, as long as they were not giants, or Philistines. Let's just say, Saul had "people." Abner was the commander of Saul's army, and he did not like David at all. He had felt shame ever since David had shown him up against the giant. It was nice to win, but "Moses!" Did David have to be so young and inexperienced?

David served Saul as a fighting man but was a shepherd at heart. He played soothing music and sang the psalms for the king when he felt troubled. He had often eaten at the king's table and had married into the family. David was married to the daughter of the king. Still, the old king talked about killing David. Saul had flown into a rage on two occasions and tried to pin David to the wall with a spear. It got so bad, his wife, Michal warned him that her dad was sending men to kill him as he slept. So David snuck away one night to find safety under the care of the prophet Samuel. Even so, Saul and his men traveled to the camp of the prophet to kill David. But God intervened. Instead of killing David, Saul and all his men found themselves prophesying and praising God when they approached Samuel and the school of prophets. It seemed that the spirit of the Lord made them all forget their mission.

Stand your ground

> But recall the former days in which, after you were illuminated, you endured a great struggle with sufferings. (Hebrews 10:32–33 NKJV)

Remembering the early days of your Christian life establishes a baseline by which everything else can be measured. I'm not suggesting that the simple faith of a new believer is always doctrinally correct. Nor am I suggesting that we should become stunted in our growth and refuse to move on. I am pointing to the importance of reflection. It is important to remember where we came from. It is equally important to remember the struggles we faced right after salvation. There were inner struggles against our newfound faith. We had to negotiate a surrender of self to accept this new disposition.

The early days of our new life in him were filled with victories over the habits, choices, and character of a lifetime. There were also challenges outside of ourselves. Friends, family members, coworkers, and employers all unconsciously conspired to challenge our faith commitment. But we endured.

If the early days of our Christian life were filled with so many victories, why then are our later days presented with so much compromise? Why is it so easy to defer to the old pre-grace nature? Why do things not simply get easier. It's either because we forget to remember grace or we chose to remember the wrong things. The Bible says that we are to remember the former days after we were enlightened. We are to remember the days after our eyes were opened to the gospel. Too often, believers seem to revel in the days before salvation. We entertain our friends with experiences of old as if we miss those days. When we spend our time admiring who we were before Christ, we naturally gravitate toward the behavior and tastes of the old man. Which brings us to the question: What are we remembering?

For most, the days after salvation were filled with new discovery. New life in Christ changes everything! If there is no change, chances are, new life in him was aborted. The cares of this life, thorns along the way, the hard-packed road of life, and other distractions may have intercepted the invitation of grace in your life. On the other hand, it is not hard to imagine that the enemy of our faith would do his best to stunt our growth. Whatever the case, new life in Christ changes our perspective, our character, and our interests. When we meet him, we embark on a path of new discovery, of awe and wonder. We begin a life of spiritual growth rooted in him and his word.

When the writer of Hebrews challenged believers to remember their early days in Christ, he was trying to get them reconnected to wonder and awe of life in him. Recognizing the huge change that has taken place in our lives is an undeniable personal testimony of the power of his grace. Proper perspective reminds us that he can do anything. Remembering where we began keeps us grounded where we are.

Remember when you stood your ground in a great contest in the face of suffering. I have always thought of life as a "contest." In that contest, myself and my past experiences are always my strongest competitors. There are challenges, obstacles, hurdles, visible, and invisible goals with incredible rewards for the successful life. I have always taken clear measure of myself in an effort to excel or exceed expectations. I have always felt the need to prove myself. To succeed.

Yet as Christians, we do not get to count success the same way the world does. Our success is not determined by the most points at the end of a game. Christian success has nothing to do with the goods that we are able to amass. The accolades of man are a poor measure. In the end, success is only measured by whether or not you are found standing your ground in the place that God has planted you.

Unfortunately, the world's standards and measures of success are often held fast in our own hearts and minds. This creates pressure to perform and produce in an outwardly visible way. Most of the time, the focus of this pressure is to gain the approval of man. Nothing could be more off the mark! We live in a kingdom where *the first shall be last and the last shall be first... The greatest among you is the servant of all...* We are instructed to *humble to ourselves in the sight of God, and he will exalt us in due season.* Self-promotion in the world is fine and at times necessary, but the Christian standard is to let promotion come from God. Our values have been changed, and our goals should be different. There is really no relationship between the world's measure of success and the Word's measure of success. Why would we embrace these limited standards? When we allow this to happen, we are standing on the wrong side of the contest.

When we are doing well, our pride loves to keep score. Victories won, ground gained, and public recognition for accomplishments are all like notches in the gun of an old western gunfighter. We all have a bit of pride. But pride is a poor measure of success.

At one point, I knew a church leader who was a rather successful businessman. His constant focus for the church and his pastor was the bottom line. More money at the end of the year and more people on the membership roll indicated to him that things were all right. In fact, the same man once confided that he had been willing to overlook the moral failings of a former pastor because the numbers and money were good. He simply did not want to rock the boat!

Numbers and money are nice to have, but holiness, spiritual vision, and the faith to follow God's plan are better. Our focus should be on following the plan of God for our own lives. Scripture tells us that he has good plans for us. When our focus is right, there will be numbers added to the kingdom. There will be victories won on his behalf. Everything that I find in scripture indicates that we all have a different citizenship, that our standards of practice are to be different than that of the world around us. If we allow sin to stay in the camp so that we can be enriched by the world's standards, we won't have to worry about rocking the boat; it will eventually sink by itself.

Years ago, I was close to an older pastor in my area. At that time, he had served the same church for more than twenty years and averaged only twenty-two people in attendance. I, on the other hand, had been in the pastorate for only a few years and served a church with 120 members. I began to feel a burden for this brother and started praying for ways that I could be an encourager for him. I took him to lunch one day, and as we visited, I asked, "Why have you stayed at your church all this time?" His answer was simple. "Well, brother," he said with the slow careful words of an older man, "I guess it's because this is where God wants me to be." Wow! Suddenly the Holy Spirit began to show me how useless it is to look at things from a natural viewpoint. My brother pastor was successful! He had found the will of God for his life and was happy to spend his life following God's plan. *He had learned to stand his ground.*

Consider 2 Samuel 23, which tells of David's mighty men. One of those was a man named Shammah. He encountered the Philistines at a time when all of Israel had fled before them. But not Shammah! Who knows what drove him? Who can understand his motivation? Perhaps anger and indignation rose beyond his need for self-preservation. Maybe he simply remembered the actions of a faithful God in his past. Suddenly, with great determination, Shammah took his stand against an arrogant overconfident enemy. He took his stand in a nondescript field of lentils and would not be moved. He fought the Philistines with great valor, and the Lord brought about a notable victory. That field of lentils may not have had great strategic value. It was clear that no one else cared to take a stand. Yet victory came in a humble place. A place of little visible value became a place of victory. All it took was one man who was willing to stand his ground. He was not willing to run. Incidentally, Shammah's actions are recorded in the record book of heaven for his stand in that unnamed place of little value. Your own field of lentils might be humble. It may not compare with places of note in the kingdom of God. You may not be written about in *Charisma* magazine or even make it to the local news. Yet, it will be the way you stand that is written about in heaven. You may be the Shammah of your generation. You may be that obscure figure in a humble place that accomplishes great victory simply because you stood your ground. Only God knows the lives that would have never been changed if you had not been faithful to the call of God to take your stand. *God keeps great records.*

Even though God has taught me this lesson, I have had to relearn it over and over, sometimes day by day. Success in the Christian life is finding the will of God and staying put. While there, you may have to kill a few Philistines, but it is always God who brings the victory. Considering the frequency of pastoral changes, the transient nature of many believers, and the discontent that many have in their careers, success might not be as common as we might think. *Stand your ground!*

A key component required for anyone to stand their ground is the ability to endure. "Endure hardship with us like a good soldier of Christ Jesus" (2 Timothy 2:3). Endurance has become a rare commodity in this world of easy answers and instant gratification. Modern theology suggests that with the proper confession and the right amount of faith, one can avoid hardship. It's often suggested that good and faithful soldiers of God never experience problems. That's just dumb! A good soldier is disciplined and prepared for hardship. He or she is ready to either repel the attacks of the enemy or to advance into new territory. The good soldier is thoroughly equipped for every good work. He is alert to the tactics of the enemy and will not be caught off guard. He is ready to stand in battle and is declared victorious ahead of time. God has amazing confidence in his troops.

It is accurate to believe that those most right and intent on living Godly productive lives will experience the harsher attacks. After all, they are on the front lines in the battle. Why would Satan bother with a lackluster, faithless believer that never rocked his boat? He wouldn't. Scripture is replete with examples of men and women who suffered for their faith. Hebrews 12 gives a pretty good roll call of suffering saints. Yet the admonition is to endure, fight *the good fight, and keep the faith*. Those especially called and anointed may at times find themselves in a "fire fight from hell." So how did you think we were going to fight? *It's not by might, nor by power, but by my spirit says the Lord.* I Corinthians 10:3 says, "*The weapons of our warfare are not carnal, but they are mighty through God for the pulling down of strong holds.*" There's the answer! We win because our weapons are really God's weapons. Be sure to know that the first time we run out against the enemy in our own strength we will suffer.

The only effective way to endure is to go back to the Word. Yet too often the tried and true often becomes overly familiar and unbeliev-able. We must remember that the only strength that we have is found in the Word. Old scriptures like Ephesians 6 are necessary. "*Put on the whole armor of God…so that you may be able to extinguish* all *of the flaming arrows of the evil one.*" *All means all!* If this is true, why do so many seem to have so much trouble? Why do we battle discour-agement? Why do so many feel the effects of "burnout?" Why are increasing numbers of pastors leaving the ministry and astronomical numbers of members leaving the church every year? Because it is tough! There is a battle! The devil does not like us, and he wants to bring defeat! Because we listen to the wrong voice, take the wrong advice, forget that we are called to stand, and we fail to remember that *we have been given everything that pertains to life and Godliness.* We forget that we are winners. The plans of our lives have been devel-oped by God, and our history has already been written.

Another necessary element in standing your ground is to con-tinue. Continue to do what God the Father has called you to do! "*But as for you, continue in what you have learned and have become convinced of, because you know those from whom you learned it, and how from infancy you have known the holy Scriptures, which are able to make you wise for salvation through faith in Christ Jesus*" (2 Timothy 3:14–15). Abraham continued. Moses continued. Joshua continued.

David continued. Jeremiah continued. Jesus continued. The disciples continued. Paul continued. You must continue as well. Do not give in or give up. Do not forget!

We tend to move from one revelation to another by compartmentalizing biblical truth. Rather than building *line upon line, precept upon precept*, we tend to forget yesterday's revelation, yesterday's prophecy, and yesterday's experience. Many of God's children appear to wake up in a new world every day. Even pastors seem to forget that we are to build our experience and knowledge base in the Lord. We are to continue in what we have learned. "*Take heed to yourself and to the doctrine. Continue in them, for in doing this you will save both yourself and those who hear you*" (1 Timothy 4:16).

That thing to which you have been called is the thing that you are to do. Did you hear God when he sent you to your church, to your place of service, or to your job as a layman? If you really heard him say, "Go," then you need to find the way to stay until he says "Leave." Over the years, I have served several churches. I know of only one that I chose for myself. Unfortunately, you can go to a good place of service with less than his perfect will. There is that good and acceptable place that is just beneath the perfect. Although God can redeem any situation, it is of great importance that we find God's plan and continue in that plan.

I pastored a church early in my ministry that, to this day, I am not sure I was really supposed to leave. My wife, Teri, and I endured hardship and resistance. The church struggled with finances during our first three years. The fight was constant, and we grew weary. On the other hand, in our first three months there, thirty-five people accepted Jesus. The congregation doubled in size in six months. Amazing supernatural things happened with great frequency, and the devil hated every minute of it! After three years of financial struggle, we retired debt, purchased a church van, remodeled the sanctuary, and had money in the bank. We were there five years and saw God win every battle.

Public insult and persecution were always dealt with decisively with the vindication of the Lord. Gossip and slander were exposed and the truth was established. Our little church stepped out of its struggle and was becoming a strong force in the community. Debt was paid. The church and ministry were gaining favor and positive identity in the community. We had every opportunity to win the lost and accomplish God's plan for that church and community.

Yet, Teri and I suffered a serious blow. After five years of battle and victory, we were tired. The straw that broke the camel's back fell. Hurtful suggestions came from a trusted friend. We decided that we could take no more. We threw in the towel and resigned, fully expecting the congregation to celebrate our departure. To our surprise, they tearfully and earnestly encouraged us to stay. Looking back, I am sure that I could have changed my decision, and the church would have been delighted for us to stay. Yet pride and pain would not let me admit that I was wrong. The train had left the station, and I felt that I could not stop it.

Since that time, I have learned that if you hear from God, I mean that if you know that you know you are where he wants you to be, it is worth fighting to stay. That is where you will find success. Success is not found in numbers of people or money in the bank but in knowing the plan of God and being persistent. Let God pick your field, and you stand your ground even if it's a field of lentils.

Success in ministry requires consistence, persistence, and a renewed mind. You cannot look at things the same if your mind has been renewed. The mind of Christ changes everything. With it, you can *count it all joy when you fall into diverse temptations.* You can rejoice that you have been counted worthy to participate in the sufferings of Christ Jesus. You can rejoice over one soul that was saved or a hundred. As a pastor, you get to watch as individuals and families grow in the Lord right before your eyes. You are allowed to share in the most personal of family experiences with your flock. You get to develop relationships with others that are common only to pastoral ministry. You also have the potential for any one of these blessings to cause hurt to you or your family.

Balance is key. Remember the good things. *Rejoice in all things, and again, I say rejoice.* Acknowledgment of the difficult is necessary so that we can learn. Challenges sharpen us and prepare us for the fight. Occasional study of our game tapes can be helpful if we don't dwell there. We can learn from our former difficulties. Yet we should never become so problem focused that we fail to see solutions or the blessings that we encounter daily. A successful believer learns to see things as they will be rather than as they are. That's vision!

Romans 14 says, "*Do not let your good be evil spoken of.*" This includes you and the voice of your mind. Learn to declare the truth of the Word into your own experience. Always be careful what you hear even if you are doing the talking yourself. Balance is key. "*Stand firm, let nothing move you, always give yourselves fully to the work of the Lord, because you know that your labor in the Lord is not in vain*" (1 Corinthians 15:58).

If you know you are where God wants you to be, then pick a spot like Shammah did and fight until there is no one left to fight. If you don't know you are in his will where you are, get out of town. The sooner the better. God gets to pick the patch!

CHAPTER 3

SOMETIMES IT HURTS!

Things had grown bad for the young man they called "giant slayer." It seemed just yesterday people were writing songs about him, and today he is a fugitive. David was troubled and confused by the change in circumstances. He had only attempted to serve well. He had attacked and defeated every enemy that Saul assigned him to. He had been invited into the palace to play his music for the king when he was troubled. David had even married Saul's youngest daughter. And look where he was today! On the run and in hiding from the very man that he had tried so hard to please.

Random thoughts rushed through his mind. *I should have stayed with my dad's sheep.* But that would have made him disobedient to his father, Jesse. *If only I had ignored the Philistine giant. But nobody else was stepping up… He was so offensive someone had to do something!* The simple life of a shepherd looked much better to David than it ever had. Yet in his very soul, David felt that the Lord had been in control all the while. From the time the prophet Samuel had paid his visit and poured the oil, David knew things would never be the same. Something big was ahead of him.

But today he ran. Survival depended on it. David regretted that he had visited the Priest Ahimelek. Since the priest was replacing the bread of presence on the altar with fresh bread, he saw no harm in giving David the old bread from the altar. He also gave David the sword of Goliath. After all, this was the hero of Israel who had killed the giant and married the king's daughter. When Saul heard that David had visited Nob, he ordered that the eighty-five priests of Nob be killed and their village be put to the sword. The only person to escape was Ahitub, the son of Ahimelek who ran to David to report what had happened.

David found himself on the run from Saul and hiding in the lowlands of the Judean hills near Israel's border. While there between two enemies, an unexpected thing began to happen. People! Scores of people who were in distress, in debt, or discontent gathered around David. These people took their stand with David when it made no sense. There was little to offer but danger with David, and yet they gathered. Among the discontent were warriors. In fact, in their own way, they all were!

Sometimes it hurts

> Sometimes you were publicly exposed to insult and persecution; at other times you stood side by side with those who were so treated. (Hebrews 10:33)

Insult and persecution? In the ministry? In America? In truth, the persecution that we face in the western world is on a whole different level than in other parts of the world. In many nations, Christians will lose their lives today because of the gospel. All around the world, the church is under attack. Even so, it seems that in places where the attack is more severe, there is more grace, and the church flourishes in spite of hardship. History has shown us that where the church is attacked and oppressed by the world, the church often thrives. *"Where sin abounds grace doth much more."*

There is something about a direct outside attack that brings people together. When the assault begins, the church (people) become more focused. They begin to remember who and what they are as well as their mission. Outside persecution has always resulted in growth for the church. Apparently, watching someone suffer for their faith communicates the gospel in an attractive manner. The attraction very likely comes from initial curiosity as to why someone would suffer for a cause. While it may be hard to imagine suffering as attractive, principle and conviction in an individual's life is beautiful and compelling. When a cause is worth giving your life, people take note, and there is growth. People want to be a part of something that really matters and makes a difference.

In today's church in America, persecution largely comes from within. There is nothing attractive or compelling about a bunch of bitter, bickering, backstabbing Christians. The persecution that arises is generally directed toward the pastor and his family or other church leaders. The reason for the persecution varies, but many problems arise because the church is out of harmony with the scripture.

Many of today's church leaders are not biblically qualified. Leadership positions such as deacon and elder have clear biblical qualifications, yet many churches fail to uphold those qualifications. As a result, we have naturally minded individuals directing the course of a spiritually focused entity. This compromises the church's ability to step out into areas requiring faith and dependence upon God. The bottom line turns to humanistic factors rather than faithfulness to God's plan for souls. The mission of the church becomes blurred and distorted, with tradition becoming the guiding force. Often the pastor is unable to really lead the flock. In places where the pastor insists on implementing biblical standards, the church responds well and becomes accustomed to "something new." There are frequent reports of random churches becoming examples of hope for others. Something about love the Lord and others?

I once heard a story about an elderly deacon in a country church. He had a great love for his church and took his responsibilities very seriously. Through years of study and teaching, this man had become an accomplished self-taught Bible scholar. He taught Sunday school every week, filled the pulpit in the absence of his pastor, and was held in high regard by the members of his congregation. During one of many times the church was conducting a pastoral search, he was asked by the committee, "Why don't you just put your name in the hat for the position?" Well, he replied, "Most folk listen to me while I'm a deacon, but if I became the pastor, people would stop listening and soon run me off."

Bam! Problems arise! The church is in turmoil, and we don't know why. It's the pastor's fault or the deacon's fault or the treasurer's fault or... The truth is, it is not about fault but about vision. Proverbs 29:18 says, "*Where there is no vision, the people perish.*" When we choose to look through the eyes of man rather than the eyes of God, we will suffer persecution and death as a body.

What an amazing transformation that has taken place in God's church! Remember when the apostles and early church rejoiced that they were found worthy to share in the sufferings of the Christ. Remember when they stood their ground and kept the faith when their loved ones were sawn asunder, when they were stoned or flogged or otherwise mistreated. Remember stories of when being a Christian required that you draw the symbol of a fish in the sand to identify yourself as a follower of the Christ. It was during this time that the church not only survived but thrived and became a force that brought direction to our world. Now it seems we don't have to stick around for the suffering. *Sometimes you were publicly exposed to insult and persecution; at other times, you stood side by side with those who were so treated.* Unfortunately, this would not attract many to God's church today. On the contrary, many surrender their faith, walk away from the church, and never look back when suffering arises.

In the early days of our church's recovery, accusation and attacks came in rapid succession. As new pastors, we were attacked strongly by those who had left with the former pastor. Unthinkable accusations were made. Ministry was hindered. Precious and innocent believers were driven from the church. Many times, our hearts were broken by the words of others. At times, I brought these issues before the deacon board for their information, prayer, and support. I needed to know they "had my back." Every time their replies were, "People will talk," "Leave it alone, and it will die," "If it's not true, just don't worry about it." One day, I received a call from one of the younger deacons. He had grown up in the church, stood firm in the early days of struggle and turmoil, but was apparently learning from the actions and behavior of the older deacons. This brother reported, "I have just heard devastating news. You will not believe what people are doing! They are saying things about the deacons that are simply not true. If we don't do something, there's no telling what people might think. We live here! Our reputations are at stake! This could hurt our families. We can't let this stand." As I listened to his concerns, I thought, *Wait a minute! I live here too. Why did it just become urgent at this point?*

This brother held what he called an emergency meeting with the oldest, longest-serving deacon for the purpose of squelching the rumors. Shortly thereafter, he resigned his position and left the church that he had been raised in to avoid the controversy. Righteousness ceased to matter. The church and its reputation in the community was no longer worth defending. Clearly the pastor's name and reputation was not as important to him as his own. Nothing really got serious until it was his own reputation at risk. At that point, he ran. Maybe he never read Hebrews 10:33, "*Sometimes you were publicly exposed to insult and persecution; at other times you stood side by side with those who were so treated*" (NKJV).

After all these years, I still find it interesting that the rumors and reputation-bashing did not become important until it was focused on the deacons. In truth, dishonesty and slanderous accusations are never pleasant to endure. Yet they come. The questions that arise during the attack are, will you stand? How will you stand? Is the struggle worth it? The answers to these and other questions will be found in your character, the direction you receive from the Father, and whether you know you are in the place of his choosing. If you are, it will be worth the struggle.

"*Now if we are children, then we are heirs—heirs of God and co-heirs with Christ, if indeed we share in his sufferings in order that we may also share in His glory*" (Romans 8:17). The early church developed an understanding of the Christ that allowed them to identify with him and his sufferings. They were catapulted from being fleeing cowards who would deny him to becoming willing martyrs for the cause of Christ. This happened for several reasons. First, they had been empowered with the person of the Holy Spirit. The *explosive power of the Holy Spirit* granted them the comfort they needed to believe, speak, and live the example that Jesus had set before them.

A glance at the garden on the night Jesus had such a difficult time keeping his prayer team awake is a good example of surrender to suffering. Clearly, Jesus did not relish what was to come. In fact, he expressed his own desire to the Father when he said, "*If only this cup could pass from me.*" This was no idle prayer! In his humanity, Jesus was struggling with the plan of God for his life. He saw what was to come. There in the garden, Jesus spent time on his knees before God and prayed until great drops of blood fell from his brow. After a time, he looked around for his prayer team and found them all asleep! He stirred them with his words and went back to prayer. This all happened again. But when Jesus left the place of prayer for the third time, he had yielded himself. It was not as if Jesus was ever in rebellion or resistant to the plan of God; it was that, in his humanity, he had to deal with the suffering that was to come. Remember what he said, "*If this cup could pass…but, nevertheless, not my will but your will be done.*" Jesus had done what we might call "praying through." He committed himself to the course no matter what. He had a clear vision of the plan and a clearer vision of the outcome. Hebrews 5: 8 tells us that "*although he was a son, he learned obedience from what he suffered and, once made perfect, he became the source of eternal salvation for all who obey him.*"

What if? What if Jesus had been like many modern Christians? What if, when the suffering arose, he simply looked for another church, moved to another community, or found some other way to start over? The point is that he did not. He had clear vision concerning his purpose and mission in life, and he stood his ground. His stand got him arrested as soon as his prayer time was finished. They took him to a mock trial with false accusers. He saw his closest friends flee in terror. He was beaten, humiliated, and finally crucified on a Roman cross and killed. His stand took him to the grave. Yet even during all of Jesus's suffering, God the Father had a plan. And three days later, the cross was bare, the grave was empty, and the disciples were beginning to see for themselves the results of standing despite persecution.

One of the healthiest things you can do is stand side by side with someone else. Lending your strength and prayer to another guarantees an abundant return. "*Bear one another's burdens.*" "*Strengthen the hands that hang down and the knees that are weak.*" "*Pray one for another.*" These and other verses instruct and admonish us to stand with other believers. Unfortunately, we often fail in this regard. We become isolated and, in turn, grow weak. We lose accountability and eventually refuse to even admit that we have problems. Psychologists would call this "denial." Scripture calls it a lie! We need one another. When we stand together, the enemy cannot say that we are the only one exposed to insult and persecution. His most common weapon in discouragement is telling us that we are alone in our suffering.

Take another glance at the garden. Jesus was struggling in prayer with what was about to happen. He took his disciples with him. Eleven of the twelve who had been with him through his ministry were there. They had just shared the Passover feast; he had just told them that he would be betrayed by one of them and asked them to pray. As they entered the garden, he asked the disciples to pray near the entrance, but Peter, James, and John were invited to go deeper into the garden with him. All that he asked was, watch and pray. After a while, he returned to where he had left his friends and found them asleep. "Please stand with me in prayer, the spirit is willing, but the flesh is weak." Jesus needed the support and strength of those around him. Unfortunately, the heaviness of their eyes caused them to sleep when they should have prayed. Their sleep brought discouragement when their prayers could have brought encouragement. Jesus was alone in his struggle.

At times, we can feel alone in our own struggles. No one can completely understand the problems that we face. Our closest friends and allies, at times, sleep when we would prefer them to take a stand and pray. But there is a friend who sticks closer than a brother. This friend learned obedience through his own sufferings and has promised to never leave you or forsake you. He is there in the darkness of your own Gethsemane. He walks with you through the valleys of life and lives so that he can intercede in prayer for you. What a friend, and what an example. As we learn obedience through the things that we suffer, we learn to stand with others more faithfully and consistently.

There is no way to over emphasize the need for and the importance of vision for your ministry, your church, and your family.

"*Where there is no revelation, the people cast off restraint*" (Proverbs 29:18 NKJV). The old KJV may be more familiar, "*Without a vision, the people perish.*" When the people and their leaders have no vision, they have no direction. They become destined to wander around in a wilderness until they can see. If they never see, they die. Vision from God gives us the opportunity to see things as they will be rather than as they are. The plan of God births hope and allows us to endure because we know we have not attained all that he has promised.

In junior high, I tried out for the basketball team. I was an all-around average athlete. All I really had was potential, and not much of that. As we practiced, competing for a place on the team, I found myself unable to jump as high or shoot as straight as others on the team. What I did find was that if they could not see the goal, they would not be able to make the shot. I did everything I could to keep them from seeing their goal. My hands went up strategically between their eyes and the prize. It worked! At least it did until I became too weary to keep up with these better-than-average players. They outlasted me, persistently looked for their goal, and eventually made their shots.

That is what vision will do for you. Sometimes it is as simple as outlasting the adversary. We must learn to see our situation as God has promised it to be rather than as it is. Unfortunately, too many can only see the guard. He is adept at covering our eyes so that all we can see are the problems. Yet if we can outlast him and persistently look for our goal, we will finally make our shot.

Some years ago, I had a youth pastor that resigned every Thursday. He had an uncooperative group of kids who seldom gave him due respect. They were rebellious, uncooperative, defiant, and divisive. In many ways, they mirrored their parents. Every Thursday I encouraged my friend to look ahead to what God had promised rather than stay focused on the trouble of the day. In doing so, I was reminding myself that our church was destined by God to become a loving, God-honoring blessing to one another and to the community. When we focus too much on the problems of the day, we risk missing the blessings that God is bringing.

It was during those early days that the Lord gave me a detailed vision for the future of our church. As I laid upon the altar week after week, I could clearly see a church body that was far different than our own. The Lord was laying out his design for our church as clearly as if he were unrolling a scroll. But on Sunday I was catapulted back into a church with problems and lack of all kinds. One Sunday, while preaching on vision, I declared to the congregation that I would much rather stand in our sanctuary on Monday than I would on Sunday. Monday always gave me the opportunity to see the church as it one day would be; Sunday forced me to see it as it was. Sunday was a bit of a struggle in those days. Monday always brought hope.

Learn to look at your own situation as it will be and not as it is. Scripture teaches that Abraham called those things that were not as though they were. Romans 4 says, "*Abraham believed God, and it was accounted to him for righteousness.*" We need to practice our faith before God, as well as before the difficult circumstances of our calling. We need to believe God.

It is interesting that the apostle Paul wrote in each of his epistles to the churches, "*Grace and peace to you from God the Father and our Lord Jesus Christ.*" During Bible college, I was told by my young professor that this was simply a traditional greeting of the time. That may well be. But I believe the words *grace and peace* carry more weight than a simple, "Hello, how ya doin?"

Grace is where we begin. It is by God's grace that we are saved through faith. Without grace, there would be nothing for us. Peace carries more meaning than an absence of conflict. Peace is the place where the blessings of God are free to flow. "*Be anxious for nothing, but in everything by prayer and supplication, with thanksgiving, let your requests be made known to God; and the peace of God, which surpasses all understanding, will guard your hearts and minds through Christ Jesus*" (Philippians 4:6–7 NKJV). Peace is beyond our natural comprehension. We can enjoy the peace of God even if conflict rages around us. Paul declared that we should have our "*feet shod with the preparation of the gospel of peace.*" Peace is at least a part of our protective armor.

While writing this chapter, I heard a nationally known pastor interviewed on Christian radio. The interviewer asked, "What is the most significant thing you have learned from your years in the ministry?" The pastor replied, "I'm not sure how significant this is, but *sheep bite!*" I believe that this is extremely significant. It instantly reminded me that I was not alone in my experience. Everyone from the local pastor to those on the national level have commented on this phenomenon from time to time. We chuckle when we hear the term "*sheep bite,*" but I'm sure we do not laugh when we are alone.

Matthew 7:15–20 reads,

> Watch out for false prophets. They come to you in sheep's clothing, but inwardly they are ferocious wolves. By their fruit you will recognize them. Do people pick grapes from thorn bushes, or figs from thistles? Likewise, every good tree bears good fruit, but a bad tree bears bad fruit. A good tree cannot bear bad fruit, and a bad tree cannot bear good fruit. Every tree that does not bear good fruit is cut down and thrown into the fire. Thus, by their fruit you will recognize them.

Luke 10:3 states, "*Go! I am sending you out like lambs among wolves.*"

Acts 20: 28–31 says,

> Keep watch over yourselves and all the flock of which the Holy Spirit has made you overseers. Be shepherds of the church of God, which he bought with his own blood. I know that after I leave, savage wolves will come in among you and will not spare the flock. Even from your own number men will arise and distort the truth in order to draw away disciples after them. So be on your guard! Remember that for three years I never stopped warning each of you night and day with tears.

Without a doubt, Jesus wanted his disciples to know that they would not always be well received. He had been the victim of the religious crowd from the day he read from the prophet Isaiah in the synagogue in Nazareth. His warnings were not fatalistic or final. It was simply, "Be careful guys." Years later, Luke, the physician, recorded the apostle Paul's warning, "Savage wolves will come in among you and will not spare the flock." His concern was for the welfare of the genuine sheep. His experience and revelation had taught him to warn those who were to follow him in ministry. If it looks like a sheep and sounds like a sheep, it still might not be a sheep. Jesus called them "wolves in sheep's clothing." Today he might have called them wolves in camouflage.

This has been an issue throughout church history. Yet today it seems that wolves in the church are on the increase. The American church, where it costs very little to be a Christian, may have become a haven for cleverly disguised wolves. We have all had people leave our churches to go somewhere else and leave somewhere else to come to us. Scripture tells us to "know those who labor among you." Despite this admonition, I can count on one hand the number of pastors over the years who have called me for a reference on their new members. The unwitting pastor usually waits until he has been bitten before he decides to "know those among his flock." I am not in favor of keeping people out of our churches. However, I am wary of wolves that slip in to do damage to the flock.

Entrance into the church has never been hard. Jesus did the hard work on the cross. Even so, we have dumbed down the requirements. At some point, we began to accept those whose lives had never been changed. In fact, about all that most pastors and churches require is that a person speak our (Christian) language.

When you accept those whose language is right but have no evidence of relationship with Jesus, you may be growing a flock of bilingual wolves. Salvation is the only thing that will change the old into the new. Sadly, today's church may be experiencing as much socialization as it is salvation. Fruit inspection is the only way to tell. Counterfeit Christians can only play the game for so long without being detected. True repentance, forgiveness of others and self, as well as the progressively sanctified life are all good fruit. On the other hand, bitterness, unforgiveness, meanness, and arrogance are all indicators of spoiled fruit or tares among the wheat.

We have forgotten the warnings of Jesus. The urgings of Paul and even the exhortation of Jude have been ignored, and we have dropped our guard. As our experiences changed to more of a social gospel, the old warnings must have seemed outdated or unneeded. Our seeker-sensitive, user-friendly approach to the gospel must maintain a firm grasp upon the truth of the Word. Without a change of heart, a soul is still lost, the unregenerate is still a sinner, and their destination is hell.

Lest I seem too harsh toward those in church, I recognize this is a well-laid plan of the enemy. His goals are, water down the gospel, wear down the faithful, turn relationship into religion, pervert the Word of God, distort the truth, disturb the sheep, and keep them from their God-given nature. There is nothing more unbecoming than a child of God indignant because of the truth and integrity of the scripture. There is nothing more disturbing than hearing one of the redeemed say something like, "I don't care what the Word says." Often people will say, "I love you," but they can tear your heart to pieces and then go enjoy their day. Extreme, right? Nevertheless, the landscape is littered with the lives of precious lambs of God who have been ruthlessly abused by godless churchgoers.

These Christian characteristics are not Christian at all. Unless… the cannon of scripture closed too soon. Which, by the way, "I doubt." Our standard for conduct is easily found in the pages of scripture. Over and again, the Word admonishes and instructs us regarding our conduct. Yet today's church is plagued by non-scriptural behavior. Men demand that the agenda for the Lord's church be changed to accommodate the whims of those who care less about his directives than they do their own likes and dislikes.

> Lord, who may dwell in your sanctuary?
> Who may live on your holy hill? He whose walk
> is blameless and who does what is righteous, who
> speaks the truth from his heart and has no slander

on his tongue, who does his neighbor no wrong
and cast no slur on his fellow man, who despises
a vile man but honors those who fear the Lord,
who keeps his oath even when it hurts, who lends
his money without usury and does not accept a
bribe against the innocent. He who does these
things will never be shaken. (Psalms 15)

There are six things the Lord hates, seven
that are detestable to him: haughty eyes, a lying
tongue, hands that shed innocent blood, a heart
that devises wicked schemes, feet that are quick
to rush into evil, a false witness who pours out
lies and a man who stirs up dissension among
brothers. (Proverbs 6:16–19)

In 1992 the news of the day was "mad cow disease." England
and the continent of Europe had been hit by this infectious disease.
Livestock was destroyed in a wholesale fashion. In days, the wealth
of generations was killed, burned, and buried. Precautions were
taken around the world to prevent the spread of "mad cow." Even
in America, air travel passengers were questioned concerning where
they had been. Those who had been to infected parts of the world
had their shoe soles disinfected. The disease has not been eradicated,
only controlled. The cost was great. Many people lost everything as
their governments attempted to stem the spread of the disease.

There is another plague affecting the fields of the world. It has
been given little press and has, in fact, been promoted rather that
snuffed out. It is the "mad sheep" problem. This insidious infection
has cost the lives of thousands through the history of the church. It
has infected the spiritual lives of tens of thousands and has cost many
their entrance into the kingdom. Think of it! Precious souls going to
hell because of a curable disease.

"Mad sheep" comes from the sin of rebellion and the refusal
of some to live repentant and holy lives. It is propagated through
close contact with the infected. It is primarily an airborne disease

that seems to be transferred from one to another by vocal vibration to the tiniest parts of the ear. Precautions include earplugs, quarantine, and daily inoculations (exposure to the vibrations of personal prayer, repentance, holiness, and the Word of God). Eradication could occur. The complete cure for this affliction was discovered around two thousand years ago in the Middle East. The cure was literally a Godsend. Individuals reaching to the highest levels have applied the necessary treatment and found it effective. Instead of killing hundreds of thousands to eradicate the disease, only one had to die. He was not even infected. Yet it was determined that his death could provide the antidote and healing for all the world. Sadly, many needlessly live with the terrible symptoms of this disease.

Jack

Many years ago, an older gentleman in our community gave me a feist puppy. He was a direct offspring of the best squirrel dog in the county. Boy, did I have plans! I began to prepare a pen for him away from the house. This was "my" dog. He would be nothing like the cockapoo or Maltese my wife had. He was a purebred "hunting dog." Smart, un-pampered, and to be feared by all squirrels. After working on the pen for a while, I took a break to cool down. When I walked in the house, I was greeted by one of my daughters cradling my fierce hunting dog in her arms with a bandana around his neck. I was then informed by my daughter that he was much too small to live so far from the house and that she would care for him. Later that evening, a summer thunderstorm arose that included great flashes of lightning and booming thunder. At every rumble, the new puppy would bury his head further into my daughter's arms. If she was not near, he would howl as if the devil himself had him by the tail. My brave hunting dog was afraid of loud noises. It wasn't a good look for a hunting dog.

A week later, a timber man in the church stopped by the house with a new pet for the girls. He handed them a small box containing a baby squirrel found in a fallen tree. From that point, every time Jack the Squirrel Dog looked in the direction of Sam the Squirrel, he heard, "No! Jack, no!" My well-bred hunting dog was pampered, fearful, and completely conditioned to stay away from squirrels. In short, he was useless for the purpose intended. He was also pretty dumb!

After a time, we were preparing to move to another city where it would be difficult to keep all our pets. The squirrel was gradually returned to the wild, and Jack was given to some neighbor boys. The first day in his new home, Jack found a pit bull chained to a tree next door. Apparently, he thought it would be a good idea to go over and establish his authority. He just wasn't very bright. Later that day, one of the young men came over to see if my daughter could coax Jack out from under their house. He was a bloody mess. He was injured so severely it was questionable whether he would live. He needed emergency medical attention. To my daughter's shock and dismay, the young man bound Jack's wounds with duct tape and laid him in a box in his laundry room. As relieved as I had been to be rid of my useless hunting dog, I had no choice but to retrieve him from his new owners and take him to the vet.

Jack lived but was never the same. His tendency toward fear turned to paranoia. If you touched his hinder parts, you were in jeopardy. Many times, after his trauma, he bit the very hands that delivered him from the duct tape and saved his life. He had no appreciation. He was grumpy and useless, but he was loved. When Jack died years later, the whole family mourned his passing. It was like losing a close family member.

Jack's story is important to me because it helps me to continue to love the biters in the congregation. They are not what they were created to become. They walk in fear. Sometimes they make unwise choices and at times seem useless for the cause for which they were born. They snarl at and bite the very hands that removed the duct tape of their lives. Still there is hope. The word and the spirit of God still have the power to change a ruined, useless life. We see it every day. In fact, we ourselves are living proof that God can save and change a life.

CHAPTER 4

COMPASSION AND JOY

The David that everyone knew was a bold man of action. The first introduction most folks had, came when David accepted Goliath's challenge. They admired his courage, were amazed at his victory, and surprised by his attitude afterward. He seemed sincerely humble. Oh, he was caught up in the excitement of Israel's victory that day, but when people began to shout the praise of the "giant slayer," he seemed to be a bit embarrassed. What they didn't know was that David felt alone and a little confused. His older brothers seemed to resent him at times. The old prophet, Samuel, had confused him, and his dad just quietly watched him. It was as if he wanted to see how David would apply the lessons of life. Jesse had always emphasized things like integrity, honor, and trust in the Lord. His favorite saying seemed to be, "We should always be willing to do the right thing no matter the cost." David had learned to apply these lessons in the dark nights as he had watched over the sheep. It seemed that when he stood in the right place, there was help beside him.

The quiet hillside at night was where David felt the most peace. It was where he learned to apply the lessons of his youth. Watching over the sheep taught him to be alert. It was also where his thoughts swirled through his mind. Somehow, in those quiet Judean nights, David felt closer to the Lord. Songs of praise to the Lord of creation filled his heart. He learned to play music on those quiet hillsides, and his audience seemed to like it. David learned that his worship ordered his thoughts, comforted the sheep, and warned the predators that he was there. Even so, there was the occasional lion or bear that would arrive, and David would step to the fight.

Tonight David sat on a hillside apart from camp to think, to pray, and to play his music and worship the Lord in his confusion. It still seemed that there was help right beside him. David found himself missing the long nights of watching over his dad's sheep. Suddenly it was as if the Lord dropped a thought in his heart. "You still are!" His heavenly Father had begun to gather a flock around him in the most unexpected way. The Father's sheep were the broken, bruised, indebted, and discontent men and women of Israel who had nowhere else to turn. The madness of their king had hurt many of the very ones who had served him. Saul grew more demanding and dangerous every day, and his behavior pushed these people toward David as sheep who needed a shepherd. That was something David knew how to do.

Compassion and joy

> For you had compassion on me in my chains, and joyfully accepted the plundering of your goods, knowing that you have a better and an enduring possession for yourselves in heaven. (Hebrews 10:34 NKJV)

The writer of Hebrews acknowledges the compassion required to reach out to those in prison as well as their apparent joy despite the challenges of life. *You sympathized with those in prison...* Why, sure! You read the scripture where Jesus said, "I was hungry and you fed me, I was thirsty and you gave me drink, I was in prison, and you visited me." We have great sympathy for those in prison. That is, if they are in prison for the right reasons! We are ready to feed the hungry and clothe the naked if they are the "worthy needy."

A part of the vision for our church has been to address our own mission field with more than just a word. In fact, ministering to the practical needs of people earns you the right to speak God's Word into their lives. Surprisingly, not everyone is always ready to get onboard with this kind of ministry. I have frequently been confronted with people inside and outside the church who question whether people really need food. If they do, it must be because they have been irresponsible. Perhaps they spend their money on drugs and alcohol or other vices. Why would we give freely to such undeserving people? Seldom do people acknowledge the judgmental nature of such assumptions. Sometimes people suffer hardship through no fault of their own. Sometimes people suffer hardship because of poor management or bad choices. Our job is to put ourselves in the position to reach those who do not yet know the Lord and to disciple those who do know him.

When our response to the human condition is flavored more with judgment than it is with grace, we have missed the point altogether. I don't see Jesus questioning the sinners and tax collectors about their worthiness. The woman with the issue of blood was not questioned about a possible clouded past. Bartimaeus was not refused his vision because he might look upon something unworthy. The woman caught in the act of adultery was simply told, "*Go and sin no more, your sins are forgiven you.*" Jesus addressed the needs of the moment and preached the kingdom. He then told his disciples, "*Freely you have received, freely give.*"

In truth, no one deserves or is entitled to the ministry that we offer. They may have created their own problems. They may be reaping what they have sown. But what about their families? What about their souls? Not one of us deserved to have the Son of God die on the cross so that our sins could be forgiven. Not one of us deserves the grace and forgiveness of God, yet it is freely offered. In our ministries, we should be the same. 2 Corinthians 1:4 says, "*God comforts us in all our tribulation that we may be able to comfort those who are in any trouble, with the comfort with which we ourselves are comforted by God.*"

Over the years at FAM, we have engaged in all kinds of outreach ministry. We have done everything from community prayer walks to feeding the homeless. We have conducted outreach into the schools by providing resources to students and teachers. The point is, we have been as ministry focused as creativity, resources, and the leading of the Holy Spirit will allow. Several years ago, we began FAM Street Ministry. We provided a simple sack lunch, a bottle of water, a five-minute message and prayer to those who would gather. At most every stop, "street people" wanted to hold hands to pray. It was as if they were hungry for a human touch. We found addicts, prostitutes, pimps, and pushers. Train riders from three states away knew where they could get a meal at a particular stop along the way. Occasionally, someone would give his or her heart to God. We have seen clear evidence of redeemed lives as people have come off the street, found hope in Christ, and have taken their lives back. One fellow on an old ten-speed bicycle once told me that he was a double-affiliated member of the Hells Angels, and if I ever needed "anything," just call him. I think he was offering to be the church hit man.

The FAM Street Ministry was exhausting! Many of those we so desperately wanted to rescue refused to be rescued. We found people living on the streets who had monthly pensions or disability payments direct deposited into their checking accounts; the street was where many wanted to be. With the winter months coming on, our street pastor worked tirelessly to get one older man out of his tent and settled into a warm, dry, and safe apartment. Though he had a regular pension, the rent was covered for a several months. He moved back into his tent the second week. Others had moms in the community that desperately wanted their adult child to come home. Most often, we found people who flatly refused to leave the street. Occasionally, we would find a family unit, usually a mom with children. Their situation was different, and most of the time even more desperate. More than often, Child Protective Services was already involved, and the mom was working hard to live up to their expectations. Seeing families and individuals step out of the desperate situations of life is always amazingly rewarding. But we have never seen anyone succeed without the life change that Jesus offers. Anything else is merely a temporary fix.

Over time, we gave out coats, blankets, food and water, socks, and underwear. We offered shelter where we could. We provided friendship and encouragement. Served as pastor, counselor, teacher, and cab driver. Over time, they taught us a lot! We know why they work in shifts on the street corners. We know the benefit of having a dog; they bring warmth at night and sympathy in the day. We learned that the clothes donated were often used in the campfire, and the tents were often abandoned when they moved on. The truth is, we were never there to sustain and support their lifestyle on the street. We were always there to offer them a bridge back home.

The resistance we were met with often came from surprising sources. First, the people we were trying to reach did not always want to be reached. Many of them simply loved the freedom and lack of responsibility that the street offered. The sobering truth is that there are plenty of kindhearted people that work tirelessly to keep them there. The intentions are good, but the result is a prolonged life in an unproductive and often dangerous place. They help them to get a check, a card, a phone, or government assistance with temporary housing. Rather than find them jobs, others work to get them disability payments. All of which is a poor substitute for the changed life that Jesus offers.

The FAM Street Ministry eventually evolved into FAM 180. FAM 180 is an intentional discipleship program that has become our recovery program. Through FAM 180, we reach families from every sector of our surrounding communities. When people talk about feeding the hungry, giving to the poor and giving of their time to reach those around us, it is easy to think of what we do as a sacrifice. But really? Is it a sacrifice when what we receive is far more than we ever gave to begin with? God always blesses our giving, blesses our efforts, and blesses our "sacrifice." He is blessing our church beyond the statistical norm that says established churches in America are in decline today. Evangelistic enthusiasm has swept over young and old alike in our congregation. Even our senior adults have embraced our contemporary style of worship and presentation of the gospel because they see God moving in the lives of the young people.

Hebrews 10:34 says, "*You joyfully accepted the confiscation of your property because you know that you yourselves had better and lasting possessions.*" Who were these people? It looks like they would get hit in the face with a big fist and simply turn around and say, "Hit me again!" What kind of foolishness is this? Isn't it taking things a bit far to turn the other cheek? Just because Jesus said to do it doesn't mean we have to, does it? Well? Honestly! It is one thing to sympathize with others when they suffer, but we never really plan on suffering ourselves. Personal suffering, no matter what the source, is unexpected and undesired.

When we consider church history and even persecution of the church in many places today, our problems pale in comparison. Seldom are our lives in jeopardy for the gospel's sake. Rarely are we forced to flee in a general dispersion like the early church. Our public meetings are relatively secure, and our people are free to come and go without fear. In the North American Church, we are so far removed from genuine persecution that inconvenience and responsibility often become a great burden. This is not to say that there are no problems. We have personality conflicts, misunderstandings, hurt feelings, unrealistic expectations, mean-spirited church members, and accident-prone pastors. We have people who long ago decided not to submit to the Lord, his Word, or those that he placed in positions of authority. And we have those who began well, really love the Lord, and firmly believe that they must make their own style preferences as sacred as the scripture.

The apostle Paul had his difficulties. He encountered his sorcerers and silver smiths. People were angered when new converts turned away from the sin of sorcery. There was no need for the household idols and trinkets produced by the silver smith. Paul's close friend named Demas had forsaken him and left the ministry. A young intern named Mark became home sick in the middle of a mission trip and cried to go home. When Barnabas left to take Mark home, he and Paul had a falling-out! And though we do not know what it was, Paul suffered from his own "thorn in the flesh."

On the other hand, Paul did not have deacon meetings, business meetings, and Sunday school. He did not have an annual budget, leaking roofs, and church vans to repair. He did not have a wife and children to care for during times of crisis. He only had stoning, shipwreck, beatings, and imprisonment. He suffered snake bite, hunger, and lack. He was rejected by many, falsely accused by some, arrested, and threatened. *And through it all, he heard from God!*

He heard from God that he was to go into Macedonia. Paul heard from God as he recovered from a stoning. He and Silas heard from God together in the middle of a Philippian jail cell. Paul heard from God while he was a Roman prisoner chained to one guard after another. In fact, it was from his prison cell that he heard from God and penned the Pastoral Epistles. Paul was free to carry on unhindered ministry in the fulfillment of his calling because he ministered wherever he was. The apostle John heard from God in exile on the rugged Island of Patmos and penned *the Revelation of John.* James, the pastor of first church Jerusalem, heard from God as his church body fled the city. The power of God on these lives and ministries is evident regardless of their circumstances simply because they had heard from God. Disciples of Jesus, one by one throughout the history of the church, have heard from God in their struggles and in their times of peace.

Think back to the times that you had heard the voice of God. What was happening in your life? Were things going well, or were there rough waters ahead? Were you able to handle situations as they arose, or had you come to the end of your rope? Were you desperate for an answer and willing to hold on until that answer came? When we get quiet long enough, when we still the restlessness of our hearts, and wait upon the Lord, he always comes through. *"They that wait upon the Lord shall renew their strength."* His word is always true. Yet this is a lesson that must be learned over and over. Our spiritual stamina must be maintained, and our spiritual memories must be jogged. It is important that we practice living as submitted and surrendered sons before God. Remember, our human nature is to go it alone until we can go no further. Isn't it great that we have not been called to get by with our human nature? We have been changed.

Much of our problem today is that we are so busy and in such a rush we have grown unaccustomed to the voice of the Lord. His comfort and counsel during our storm are often missed. Because of this, we are too often ill-equipped to deal with problems as they arise. Yet it is problems and persecution that tend to keep people prayed up and knowing their only hope is in God. The desperation that arises from persecution forces us to depend upon the steady hand of God for our very survival. It is during the bleak times that his voice is often heard most clearly. If only we would learn to hear from him in the quiet of the day when we are not desperate! What joy would rise in our hearts from the ability to visit with our heavenly Father as Enoch did. What amazing peace and confidence abides in the life of one whose relationship with the Father is fresh. Psalms 42:1 says, "*As the deer pants for the water brooks, my soul thirst for God.*" Even here in this passage, David is troubled by the contempt of others.

When we see the needs of others or face trouble as a body, the church is great at rallying together for support and encouragement. We give. We defend. We cover, and we comfort. These are the times we really shine in our personal sacrifice for others. When we rally together in times of distress, we often succeed in our mission of the day because we have heard the voice of God. But what would we sacrifice of self in peaceful days? What do we do to maintain our relationship with the Father?

In our early days of salvation, we died to self. We surrendered our old lives, walked away from old friends, and closed the door on our past. The change that salvation brought was dramatic and dynamic. We learned to pray and study his word. We felt comfort from his presence and drew strength by his spirit. But after a while, we grew accustomed to the "new life." Salvation became common to our experience, and the need to die daily faded into the background of our lives. Our desperation for God generally rises and falls based upon need. Personal time given in prayer, Bible study, and other spiritual disciplines becomes a challenge. Thankfully, this life provides plenty of challenges.

CHAPTER 5

HANG ON TO YOUR CONFIDENCE

One of those days!

Have you ever had one of those days where you had to go somewhere you did not want to go and support someone you really did not want to support? That was the day that David was having.

Saul's relentless pressure on David and his followers kept them constantly on guard and on the move. From the cave of Adullam to frontier border towns to the rugged hillside, David was never able to relax. He did not want to engage Saul's army. Their numbers were greater. Many were friends who David had fought beside. They were a part of his beloved Israel, and David was sure that he did not want to touch the man that God had anointed to be the king. David was having more trouble convincing his men not to kill Saul. In fact, Saul's arrogance and carelessness placed him in reach of David's most ardent supporters more than once. Something had to change! Clearly, it was not going to be Saul.

Finally, David along with his men and their families moved into Philistine territory in their effort to stay out of Saul's reach. David with his six hundred fighting men allied themselves with Achish, the king of Gath. After a time, David approached the king and asked for a town in the countryside where he, his men, and their families could live. Achish gave David the town of Ziklag as their base. David and his army spent their time raiding the enemies of Israel.

They raided the Gesurites, Girzites and the Amalekites, but had the Philistine king thinking they raided southern Israel. Their raids left no one alive to report and left no sign that David was the attacker. Every time David returned from a raid, he would share with Achish a portion of the spoils and lead him to believe that he had raided southern Judah, the Jerahmeelites, or the Kenites. Achish was sure that Israel was developing a deep hatred for David and his men... It became easy for Achish to believe that David would have no option but to serve him. All the while, David was attacking Israel's enemies and Philistine allies.

But today was different. David had feared this day would come, and he was stuck. Spring had come. It was the time of year when kings went to war, and the Philistines were about to war against Israel. David had no choice but to present himself to Achish and commit his fighting men to the battle against Israel. He was obligated. He had no other choice. So here he was. We will never know what actions David may have taken in the battle. It's likely he would have turned upon his Philistine benefactors and fought to defend Israel. Ultimately, that's what the lords of the Philistines thought. They were convinced that David would turn against them in battle. They well-remembered the David that they had faced in previous battles. So they instructed Achish to send David and his fighting men home to Ziklag.

There was no way to describe the relief that David and his men surely must have felt that day. They had kept up the charade that they were enemies of Israel without striking a blow. They still had a home out of Saul's reach. It was turning out to be a good day! At least until they saw the smoke.

Hang on

Therefore do not cast away your confidence,
which has great reward. (Hebrews 10:35 NKJV)

We have all seen weariness, burnout, disappointment, and disillusionment among pastors, leaders, and church members. One of the challenges of building a great church for God is found in your definition of a great church. If a "great church" is one bursting at the seams with people, always having an abundance of money, being number one in missions giving, all while in a successful building program, you might still be looking in the wrong place for greatness. To be sure, anyone might want any or all the above, but what is the motive? Greatness in God is not measured by the number of attendees or the size of the budget. He did not say that "I am only coming back for the biggest and the richest!" He said, "I am coming for a bride that is without spot and wrinkle or any such blemish." He is coming back for a clean church. A clean church can be found among the largest and strongest, the newest or the oldest.

Many older churches, however, have developed personality traits and family characteristics that are contrary to the word and counterproductive to growth. Inbred traditions and dysfunctional power structures can make it very difficult for a pastor to pastor. When God's people are set in their ways, it can surely present a challenge. Because of these and other factors, today's church growth experts insist that older established churches are generally in decline and that the best way to grow a church is to plant a new one. This position almost seems to grant permission for failing churches to fail. "We are in decline because we are statistically destined to do so." This may be a good excuse, and it may bear out with natural observation, but it's not a good reason to give up on the great commission or God's church. At its core, most every church would love to grow. The problem comes with accommodating new people and new ideas, new trends at the expense of the biblical standard. The pastor is faced with the choice of either going with the flow, look for a better church, or challenging the dysfunctional and unscriptural attributes of the church he is in and working to bring change. Most of America's pastors are serving in established churches, and I don't think we should be so ready to throw in the towel on the mission we have been given. Churches and people can change.

In every way, the church and the family are alike. The Bible clearly uses the imagery of marriage to illustrate the church and in turn uses his love for the church to illustrate his love for the family. The relationship of Christ and his church is directly compared with the relationship of a husband and a wife. Yet our day is filled with throwaway churches and throwaway families. Our definition of "great families" has been rewritten by our society. Our world has prepared us to embrace failure in our marriages. If there is challenge, decline, discontent, or disagreement, just go find another. God's people change churches without ever having developed a relationship with the first, second, or third. If I am challenged, I'll change. Husbands and wives often give up on their marriage with the same disregard. Principles like patience, forgiveness, unconditional love, peace, and joy are no longer embraced. The average length of a marriage in the United States today is 8.2 years. The overall divorce rate is in the mid 50-percent range. Situational and seasonal spikes in divorce have been identified, and more older Americans are divorcing than ever. And why not? Very little matters if the foundational principles of our lives (biblical standards) are no longer valid.

However, there is always a *however*. If we would allow the Lord to grow us, mature us, and develop us in him, we would grow in our ability to demonstrate biblical characteristics. Jesus changes us, discipleship grows us, and his spirit leads us. He never leads us contrary to his word. He really does have a plan for our lives.

Don't throw away your confidence. Confidence is a funny thing. It comes and goes in people's lives like waves on the seashore. One day we are full of confidence and know that anything is possible; the next day, circumstances have rocked our world, and we just don't know what to expect. Israel experienced the confidence rollercoaster over and again. In fact, God anticipated their inconsistency and chose their route toward the land of promise accordingly. "*Then it came to pass, when Pharaoh had let the people go, that God did not lead them by way of the land of the Philistines, although that was near; for God said, "Lest perhaps the people change their minds when they see war, and return to Egypt"* (Exodus 13:17 NKJV). One day they left Egypt with "great boldness." The next, they were wishing for the security of their captivity. They crossed the Red Sea in victory, only to long for the sweet water of Egypt on the other side. The children of Israel threw away their confidence over and over.

Don't we do the same? We hear the voice of God. We know that he has a plan for our lives and has given us direction. We go to a new church, launch a new project, embark on a new adventure, and suddenly God changes his mind. Or so it would seem. We change course, cancel projects, and change churches. Problems arise. The people complain. They are reluctant to embrace the "new vision." Discouragement comes in, and we throw away our confidence. "Maybe I didn't hear him." "Perhaps I was wrong." "Certainly, things would be easier if I was in God's will." "I'll go somewhere else and try something new." This behavior occurs in many of our people as they move from church to church. It also drives pastors to move from one pastorate to another and our people from one job to another. The concept of steadfast is missing in our lives. There is no question that it is the Lord's prerogative to move us wherever he wants. I just think we probably move more frequently than he does. Sometimes we might "*change our minds when we see war, and return to Egypt.*"

Our spiritual confidence comes through him. It is secure in our salvation and calling as children of God. When we know who we are in him and can say Like Paul, "*I know whom I have believe,*" we can easily hold fast to our confidence in the specificity of our calling. Are you an apostle, prophet, evangelist, pastor/teacher? Your calling will dictate your stance. Are you a missionary church planter, an evangelist, or a pastor? Each will have different assignments. Today I believe that we need a resurgence of pastors who are willing to stake their claim to God's plan for their lives and stand their ground. Our churches need men and women of confidence who will hold fast to their confidence when they see the war. Only then will we begin to see the church that has been in decline begin to turn around. Bear in mind that when we speak of the church, we are not talking about bricks and mortar. God's people are the church. Flesh and blood. It is his plan to place his hope for the church in the heart and soul of his people.

There are many elements needed for a church to be successful in our day, but the most important is a confident pastor. A confident pastor will eventually produce a confident church. Confidence in the Lord will help you in the battles. Confidence will enable you to stand when others may flee. Confidence in the Lord will allow for the establishment of long-term ministries that are necessary for our churches to become successful. Confidence in the Lord will provide the opportunity to address weaknesses and character flaws in the local church that stifle growth. It is our confidence in the Lord that enables us to risk believing, *"I can do all things through Christ who strengthens me"* (Philippians 4:13 NKJV). I suppose the best question to ask is, "Do I have confidence that I am where the Lord wants me to be?" If the answer is yes, then God will grant vision and anointing for that specific place.

Many new churches have been started from the ruins of a church that has split in the face of this challenge. Splits occurs because (1) pastors do not always act with good judgment, patience, and godly motives; (2) congregations do not always respond with good judgment, patience, and godly motives; (3) many leaders (pastors, deacons, elders) really do not have the resolve to insist, "We will follow God and his word." When this is the case, something less than the will of God is born.

On the other hand, many God-ordained churches have developed habits and traditions that limit their effectiveness. If you find yourself in a traditional, stilted, stagnant church that is tightly controlled by the most carnal men possible, it is not your responsibility to change that church. It is God's church! It is his word that brings the power, and it is by his spirit that he chooses to move. Your responsibility is to have the confidence that he can do what his word declares. Remember, *"some plant, some water, but it is God that gives the increase."* It is God who brings the change. You should pray for change, preach for change, take an appropriate stand in the face of ungodliness, and love your people. Many will not like it! Some will leave! Others will become slanderous gossips that want you to move. But if you know that you are called to your church, you must be willing to stand and remind yourself that this is God's church, and the outcome is his responsibility, not yours.

This is where *do not throw away your confidence* becomes a necessity. Did God call you to your church, or was it just a job? As a layman, did God call you to your church, or are you just passing through? If he called you, you can have confidence. If he did not, pack your bags! If you have a genuine call, and you have spent quiet time alone with the Father, he has begun to give you vision for that church and ministry. I know this because God the Father does not tease his children. He would never give you a job assignment without giving a job description to go with it. You may see the short-term vision or the long-term vision, but rest assured that the hopes and dreams that have grown in your spirit are not figments of your imagination (assuming mental stability and biblical agreement).

After a while, the best of us feel the effects of the struggle, especially if we have been assigned an older church. Change does not occur fast enough. Frustration sets in. Confidence begins to slip, and there you go. At the same time, we read excellent books on church growth that reinforce the statistical demise of the older churches. If you are normal, you soon wonder, "Why didn't I get to go to the site of the next trouble-free mega church?" Before long, résumés go out, the moving truck is called, and you find yourself pastoring the same church in a different location with different people who have the same issues.

This is where hanging on to your confidence comes in handy. Hanging on to your confidence lets you benefit from God's timing. Timing is always important. As I wrote earlier, the church that I pastor had a long history of adversarial relationships between the pastor and the deacons. A review of old business-meeting minutes helped me to track this behavior back through several long-term pastorates before mine. It had been the custom of the board to fight and oppose the pastor, limit his effectiveness, limit his ability to invest in ministry tools, and at the same time demand outward results. I know of one pastor who had to take a swig of Maalox before his board meetings. When the board room door closed, the yelling began.

In my second board meeting in this new church, I was verbally whipped by one of the deacons. I had never been subject to such treatment in previous churches. So I made it my mission to understand these men. I assumed that their behavior was left over from previous bad experiences and that as they grew to know me, things would improve. We shared fellowship meals, prayed, and read devotional material before each meeting, and about every other meeting, they would "plow my field," i.e., treat me badly. At the same time, the Lord was insistent that I hold my peace and not engage in the fight.

Understand, it was not every deacon that instigated this behavior. In one particularly harsh board meeting, one deacon stood over me in a threatening manner, almost nose to nose, demanding that I do as he instructed. It was so bad I was compelled to stand up and face him down. There was nothing physical, but in the heat of the moment, I would not have been one bit surprised if he had hit me. What did happen, however, was that I stepped down to his level of behavior. My reaction lowered me in the eyes of several in the room. I had been set up. From there, things only got worse.

About my third year in this church, a quiet but seriously spiritual man was elected to our board. He had been a witness to the previously mentioned event and yet had said nothing. Sometime around his sixth month on the board, he looked sternly across the table at a long-term deacon and said, "Brother, I took you aside privately after your last outburst and discussed your behavior. Now I rebuke you publicly! You have no right or reason to speak to our pastor that way!" We were all momentarily dumbstruck. No one in the room had seen anything like this before. I instantly knew that I liked it.

Regardless of what one might assume, my brother's rebuke had little effect on the overall behavior of the perpetrator. He was quietly egged on by another deacon who diligently worked behind the scenes. Their goal was to goad me into another inappropriate response and further damage my credibility. However difficult it was, I became more determined than ever to honor the Lord with my responses to their mistreatment. Knowing I had an ally in the room helped.

Near the end of my fourth year, I had long since stopped feeding the deacons. Something about them eating my food and verbally abusing me in the same meeting didn't seem right. One Sunday afternoon, we held a meeting that went rather well. We had made some progressive decisions, when at about 5:50 p.m., a verbal explosion erupted. I found myself hurled from a peaceful productive meeting into the worst tongue-lashing yet. It seemed as if the majority of the deacons were suddenly opposed to me, and all was lost. Surprisingly, they disregarded the tape recorder in the center of the table and went "enthusiastically nuts." It was so bad two of the deacons and I sat there with our mouths open in disbelief. To make matters worse, this occurred ten minutes before our Sunday evening service. As I regained control of the room, I felt the Lord say, "It's time!" As I prepared to dismiss the board, I called a meeting for the next evening for the purpose of addressing their behavior.

I prayed most of that night and the next day. All I know is that I felt it was God's time to directly address the issue. I also was determined that no matter how things went, I would no longer live with this kind of treatment. God had shown me that their behavior, although directed at me, had little to do with me individually. Realizing that it was not personal didn't necessarily make it easier, but it did allow me the freedom to pray without personal offense. Oh, I was offended. I was offended that the church was held hostage, offended that the principles of the Word were ignored. I was offended that distraction and division among the leadership kept us from reaching our community.

I had learned that there was a long-term spiritual stronghold that had attached itself to the board of our church and created division among the leaders. At least two of my predecessors had endured the same treatment. I had prayed specifically about our need for a couple of years and was still standing when the Lord said, "It's time!" His timing is imperative.

The next day, I developed a document outlining pastor-board relationships, calling, and responsibilities. I included scripture focusing on pastor and deacon selection, calling and character, excerpts from the constitution and bylaws that dealt with the pastor and official board's working relationship. The last page was an agreement/adherence statement. It reads as follows:

> I understand the office of deacon is a position of responsibility that requires the highest adherence to the standards of scripture. I am to function peaceably, with integrity, with hon-

esty, and a sincere desire to bless those around me. I know the success of the ministry depends upon the relationship between the pastor and the board. The scriptures, as well as the constitution and bylaws give specific guidance concerning my responsibility, calling, conduct and authority.

I commit myself to live and function within the bounds established by scripture and defined in the constitution and bylaws. If I find myself unable to fulfill my calling, support my pastor, or be a blessing to my church, I will resign and allow another to take my place.

Signed: _____

Date: _____

What followed was not pretty! On the other hand, four of the seven deacons immediately agreed to the wisdom of the scripture and the guidelines of the bylaws. After lengthy discussion, I dismissed the meeting and instructed the board to spend the next two weeks praying about their decision. The following Wednesday, three deacons resigned rather than submit to the standard set forth in scripture. The adversarial spirit was broken, and the remaining members of the board adopted the practice of reviewing the document annually as well as requiring deacon candidates to sign in agreement prior to being approved to serve.

Behold, how good and how pleasant it is for brethren to dwell together in unity! It is like the precious oil upon the head, running down on the beard, The beard of Aaron, running down on the edge of his garments. It is like the dew of Hermon, descending upon the mountains of Zion; For there the Lord commanded the blessing—Life forevermore (Psalms 133 NKJV.)

Hold on to your confidence when making comparisons!

New churches, mega churches, out-of-the-ordinary churches… Looking at the success of others is often a two-edged sword. Inspiration and encouragement can grow by seeing others succeed. On the other hand, comparing our own experience with those of others can at times hurt rather than help. It is important to remember that there is always more to the picture than meets the eye. The successful pastor of a mega church might be an "overnight" success that was twenty years in the making. During his "overnight," he might have had to fight every demon in hell to see the victory in his church. Others may have started from the ground up with careful planning and excellent mentoring. Many of us in established churches have dreamed of all the changes we would make if we ever started a new church. A great number of successful pastors have gone into older established churches, fought the good fight, and built amazing ministries. They did this with the help of the Lord, much wisdom, and prior experience. They paid their dues.

The trouble is, I do not have the experience of a Tommy Barnett, the influence of a Jentezen Franklin, or the eloquence of a Steven Furtick. I do not pastor a new church with no predetermined bad habits. The church I pastor has been around a while. It had just gone through a split when I became the pastor. At least one of the definitions of ministry had become clouded, and the church had forgotten its purpose. The church board was accustomed to having an adversarial relationship with their pastor and saw no need to change simply because I moved into the office. Our church was fraught with bad habits, hurt feelings, spiritual and emotional wounds, unforgiveness, suspicion, and carnality. On top of all this, God called me to this church and gave me a vision. It took six years or so before our church began to embrace the vision that God had given and to begin to get on track with his plan.

Today I have been the senior pastor for twenty-four years, and in many ways, we are living what we were seeing so long ago. These years have brought peace, harmony, and a genuine sense of family within the body. We have recovered from the financial losses incurred when rebellious leaders walked out. We have repaired our testimony in our community and have enjoyed numeric, financial, and spiritual growth. We have experienced the heartache of rebellion and division and celebrated recovery from the same. It is a joy to experience the fulfillment of the vision that God gave in the midst of the fire. Who knew that the "fire" would include COVID-19? *Just a bit more, and we might just become one of those overnight success stories!*

I have wanted to quit more times than a few. Our church was a mess! But it belongs to the Lord, and he loves me enough to have me be a part of the great plan that this mess will become. The opportunity is marvelous. The progress has at times seemed slow. But the reward is rich! One day, if the Lord tarries, some young preacher will look longingly at our FAM and be slightly envious of our overnight success. When that happens, I hope to have the presence of mind to not only show him what God has done but also a little bit of where we have been.

So do not throw away your confidence. Many places in scripture relate to this single verse.

> In him and through faith in him we may approach God with freedom and confidence. (Ephesians 3:12)

> Such confidence as this is ours through Christ before God. (II Corinthians 3:4)

> We have come to share in Christ if we hold firmly till the end the confidence we had at first. (Hebrews 3:14)

> Let us then approach the throne of grace with confidence, so that we may receive mercy and find grace to help in our time of need. (Hebrews 4:16)

And now dear children, continue in him, so that when he appears we may be confident and unashamed before him at his coming. (1 John 2:28)

This is the confidence that we have in approaching God: that if we ask anything according to his will, he hears us and if we know that he hears us—whatever we ask—we know that we have what we asked of him. (1 John 5:14)

Therefore do not cast away your confidence, which has great reward. (Hebrews 10:35 NKJV)

CHAPTER 6

WHEN YOU WANT TO QUIT!

Mighty men and a kingdom

As David and his men returned to their families, the smell of smoke was heavy in the air. Different from the smell of wood smoke, from a cook fire, this was heavy and mingled with the familiar smell of destruction. In their raids, David and his men had burned villages as they fought their enemies. Now a familiar smell arose from their own homes. The closer they got, the more anxious they became. Finally, they topped the last rise. The town of Ziklag laid in ruin. Their homes had been burned; rubbish piles still smoldered, and everyone was gone! The women and children, the cattle and sheep, and anything else of value had been taken. Although David and his men had seen battle and even engaged in the destruction of towns and villages. It was different when it was their own that was destroyed. David and his mighty warriors lifted their voices and wept until they could cry no more.

When David and his men finally gathered themselves, they began to look for someone to blame. Almost immediately, some of the lesser men said, "It's David's fault! If he had not led us out, we would have been here to defend our families." The anger and grief were so strong and fresh the men became irrational and suggested that they stone David. In his distress, David cried out to the Lord and soon found himself encouraged. David and Abiathar, the priest, sought the Lord's direction. "Should we go after them? Could we overtake them?" And the Lord answered, "Go, for you shall surely overtake them and recover everyone and everything."

David and his army had not traveled far when it became clear that some of the men were weary from their journey and were slowing them down. So David pushed ahead with four hundred men and left the others to watch over their supplies. Their attackers had been the Amalekites, who had been raiding towns and villages along the border between Israel and the land of the Philistines. They were an old enemy that had long held a grudge toward David and the people of Israel. To find Ziklag unprotected was unexpected. They surmised that David and his men were busy at war, so they had nothing to worry about. Their gods had blessed them, and they had all the time in the world.

When David's scouts came upon the Amalekite camp, they found them spread out and unsuspecting. They were eating, drinking, and dancing in celebration of their good fortune. They had more wealth than they could have imagined and not a care in the world. Then David and four hundred angry Israelites showed up. David and his men fought the Amalekites from sundown until evening of the next day and recovered all that that had been carried away. David and his men rescued their families and recovered all the goods that had been taken from Ziklag. In addition, David's men took all the spoils of the Amalekite campaign.

The path of David's life led him through more than a few difficult places—from fight to flight, from hiding from his enemies to confronting them, from a cave to a kingdom. David had the experience of standing alone to face the giants of his life, as well as the joy of having others rally to his cause and stand with him. David knew the deep friendship of those who were willing to die by his side, and he knew the deep sorrow of rejection and betrayal. His life was filled with amazing success, great challenge, as well as significant failures. After a time, the words of Samuel, the prophet, were fulfilled, and David became king of Israel.

Most of those who had gathered with him in his early days still stood by his side. Just over thirty of them became known as David's mighty men. They became known as heroes among the people. Men like Adino the Eznite, who killed eight hundred men in one battle. Eleazar, the son of Dodo, fought beside David until his hand stuck to his sword and the Lord brought about a great victory. Shammah, Abishai, Joab, and Benaiah were men like others who stood their ground and made their lives count in the plan of God. Their example of courage and commitment still stands as example for men today.

Better than that, the Lord stood by his side. The relationship with God that began as a boy watching over the flocks of his dad's sheep continued to grow. The Lord chose David to lead his people when another held the throne. He stood beside him as his enemies tried to end his life. He granted clear direction when David was unsure where to turn. At every turn, the Lord was there. God identified David as a man after his own heart. The call of God and his anointing on our lives never assures ease, but following God's plan always assures success. Give it time, fight your adversaries, and keep going.

When you want to quit

Therefore do not cast away your confidence. (Hebrews 10:35 NKJV)

Persevere: persist, endure, continue, carry on…
What do you do when everything in you wants to quit? Check yourself. Check your call. Examine the source of your frustration. Examine the pattern of your own actions and behavior. Over the years, I have seen numerous individuals "throw everything away." Their actions were at times both well planned and spontaneous. I am sure I have witnessed carefully crafted schemes to discard responsibility. I also know of folks whose momentary indiscretion cost them everything. The result is the same—a lifetime of pastoral service gone overnight. The loss of one's testimony and character can occur in an instant. Planned or not, I have never known one to throw away their confidence without great regret.

On the night that Jesus and his disciples went into the garden to pray there was the temptation to quit! As they entered the garden, he asked three of his closest friends to go further into the garden as they prayed. When he looked around, everyone was asleep. They had given in to the temptation of their weariness. They had left Jesus alone in his time of greatest need. "Wake up! Can't you stay awake to help me pray?"

When we examine the prayer in the garden, it is easy to recognize and relate to Jesus's humanity. He prayed, "*If this cup could pass from me.*" In other words, "I would rather not endure what I know to be coming. If there was another way… This will not be easy… Nevertheless, '*not my will but your will be done.*'" If you and I could ever consistently come to agreement with this prayer, the question of quitting would easily be answered. Jesus didn't quit, so neither will I.

I could never over emphasize the importance of checking yourself and your calling. By checking yourself, I mean check your own heart. What is your condition? Are you fresh? Are you strong? Are you encouraged in the Lord, or are you growing weary? Emotional outlook and attitude are important factors to consider. Important life-altering decisions should never be made in the midst of emotional episodes. On the other hand, if you are not sure you are in the place of his choosing and are not genuinely called by God to ministry, why on earth would you put up with its demands? Do you have a specific call to your present place of service? There are those who found a good opportunity, ran from a bad situation, or were invited to serve by the deacons. Others know that they are God-directed, God-sent, and God-ordained for their place of service. Even then, there will be times that the prayer might be, "*If this cup could pass from me…*" If you have confidence that God placed you where you serve, you should examine your sources of frustration. *What are the real problems?* Deacons? Members? Staff? Self? Finances (church or personal)? Are there bears and lions among the sheep, or are the little foxes spoiling the vine? Knowing the source of your frustration is important.

Regardless of your personal view of psychology and emotional issues, the time will come when you will be weary and more than a little depressed. Elijah was ready to give up immediately after his most significant victory. He cried out, "I'm done! After all, I'm the only one that really cares any more. Just get me out of here even if you have to kill me to do it!" Instead of getting him out, God sent an angel to refresh him with a hot meal from heaven. His refreshing from God did not come because of his great faith or his deep prayers. The refreshing came because God was not through with his prophet.

There is the story of David taking his army out to fight only to return to an empty village. Everything was gone. The Bible says that their wives, their sons, and their daughters were taken, and the men cried until they had no more power to weep. David had lost as much or more than his men. Yet those who followed David began to blame him. Some suggested he be stoned for leading them out and leaving the village undefended. David's reaction to their unfair rush to judgment was *to encourage himself in the Lord*. Very likely, David reflected on the faithfulness of God that he experienced as a child while tending his father's sheep. The lion and the bear came out, and God delivered them into his hand. Other memories like Goliath and narrow escapes from King Saul served to remind him of God's comfort and protection in dangerous times. As he sought God in his troubles, he received direction and encouragement to pursue his enemy, rescue his people, and regain his goods. When he overtook the raiders, not only were his people returned but the plunder they recovered from the enemy enriched David and his followers alike. It is good to remember that what the enemy intends as bad, God can turn around for good. This will only work when we keep our eyes on him in our times of testing.

It is important to examine the source of our frustrations. I believe that most of the big issues we face have little effect upon our overall contentment. Big problems tend to rally the troops. When the body stands together, strengthening and encouragement usually follows. We never mind fighting for a cause when the cause is just, when we are supported by those around us, especially when we are winning.

It's the quiet times when the troops are not aroused that we weaken in our resolve. Those times that we seem alone are particularly draining. There are times we feel alone in the crowd. It is difficult for laypeople to view things from a ministry perspective. As a result, they fail to understand the pressure and weight carried by the pastor and his team. Outwardly, they declare their determination to stand, but when the "temple guard" arrives, they scatter like the disciples in the garden.

At times, the pastor is his own worst enemy. At times, mistakes are made that a bit more thoughtfulness might have avoided. *It is important to examine the pattern of our own actions and behavior.* When the heat turns up, where do we look? What is our first action when issues (large or small) arise? Are we rash? Do we speak in haste? What do we do to keep ourselves fresh? How do we respond to subtle and not-so-subtle messages from church members? Are we steady and coolheaded? Do we hold our tongue when others may not? Can we calmly hear criticism, weigh it, and reply in a careful and thoughtful manner? The answers to these and other questions will help predict our ability to stand in the place of our calling.

There are pastors who shoulder the responsibility for the rise and fall of the church. This eventually becomes a weight too difficult to bear, and they look for a way out. Why? Unrealistic expectations of the congregants, unrealistic expectations of deacons and elders, and unrealistic expectations of the pastor himself all combine to create a burden too heavy for anyone to bear.

Many congregations have surrendered their responsibility for the kingdom's work. Personal evangelism, outreach, and visitation are negligible to the rank and file. After all, that's why we pay the preacher! There are times that the deacons may adopt a bottom-line view of the church. As long as the numbers are up and the offerings are up, things are good. If the end-of-the-year financial report indicates positive numbers, all is well. If, on the other hand, spending exceeds income, watch out. No matter how big the sacred cow (savings account) is, trouble is coming. Remember the deacon who said, "I knew our last pastor was involved in immorality, but the numbers were up, and the money was good, and I didn't feel like rocking the boat." Let that same deacon serve with a pastor intent on cleaning compromise and corruption from the church and see what happens. His boat begins to rock, and he begins to work as an adversary rather than in the advisory role. Sometimes a stand for what is right costs us members. Lost members generally mean lost tithes. This shakes up the bottom-line thinkers and puts a significant weight upon the shoulders of the pastor. By the way, not all deacons are bottom-line thinkers. Some are right with God, will hold fast to his Word, walk by faith, and support their pastor.

All too often, the burden of church growth, financial stability, and congregational contentment to rest squarely upon the pastor's shoulders. Why? Because that's what so many expect. The apostle Paul points to the biblical pattern for the church in 1 Corinthians 3:6, "*I planted the seed, Apollos watered it, but God made it grow.*" God is in control when we let him be! No pastor can live long under the tyranny of unrealistic expectations. We have been called to plant and water, but God is responsible for the increase. After all, it's his plan, his church, and his strength required for it to succeed.

There is no question that the ministry is difficult. There are busybodies and Jezebels, church bosses and agitators. There are always needs. We need more teachers. We need more people. We need more money. The job is never complete. The pastor of today is expected to be preacher, theologian, and the purveyor of hidden biblical truth with the flare of T. D. Jakes and the smile of a Joel Osteen. He is expected to be a counselor, tax advisor, legal expert, accountant, and at times may be asked, "*How do I clean the rust from my BBQ grill?*" The pastor may or may not work in the sun forty hours a week. But he is always on call. When he is refreshed in the Lord, he is glad to be called. Yet the hassled, harried, tightly wound pastor, skimping on prayer and the Word, gets to his limit quickly. What's the big deal? You only work Wednesdays and Sundays.

Prescription:

1. Remember whose church you serve and who is responsible for the increase.
2. Keep your emotions, actions, and words in check. And unfortunate response to stressful stimuli can damage your character and reputation quicker than anything else. They

might not remember that you were provoked, but they will remember how you responded.

3. Pray, read the word, and stay fresh with God. Focus on him and know that he has good plans for you.

4. Pull away from the crowd. Take a break. The gospels give us multiple examples of Jesus getting away from the crowd and going into the mountain to pray. At times, he left the confrontations, the sick, the lost sheep of Israel, and even his friends for time alone with the Father.

   a. Intentional pulling away. A day off. It is important to take personal time away from the office. Sure, you can be reached for emergencies. At times, you forfeit your day off for weddings, funerals, and other ministry needs. However, if you plan consistent time off, you will be better for it.

   b. Conferences. Attend ministry events. You have no doors to unlock; the air-conditioning is someone else's problem. All you must do is relax and enjoy. You are not there to evaluate or criticize the message. You are there to be fed and blessed. Relax, let down your guard, and you might just feel a new wind in your sails.

   c. Go have fun. Golf is great, and hunting is fun. But what I mean is—take your wife and get out of town. At least once a quarter, Teri and I get away if nothing else for a night. What we do is our business, but we stay fresh. Our marriage is strong, and our ministry is strengthened. I enjoy the time spent with my best friend, partner in ministry, and wife. (They are all the same person.)

CHAPTER 7

PERSEVERANCE

David's persistent character allowed the plan of God to gradually unfold in his life. He outlived the troubles of his early years and became the king of Judah after Saul and Johnathan were killed in battle. In a day when everyone remembered the prophecies of Samuel concerning David, some chose to go their own way and appointed Saul's son, Ishbosheth, as king of Israel. Shortly after, Israel and Judah were at war.

The war might have been better defined as skirmishes. David was content to wait for the plan of the Lord to unfold. Prudence dictated that he should not create lifelong enemies of the people he was ordained to lead. David was determined to avoid all-out war with Israel. On the other hand, there were men like Abner, the commander of the army of Israel, and Joab, the commander of the army of David, who seemed to be itching for a fight. It was the same attitude that made David's men want to kill king Saul so long ago. Patiently waiting for the plan of God was not their strong suit. Yet David had learned to be persistent at a very young age. It was his persistent practice that had allowed him to protect the sheep and slay the giant. It was his persistent faith that caused him to believe the old prophet, Samuel; his persistent search for the heart of God that enabled him to write the amazing songs of the Psalms. Finally, it was his persistence in honoring the Lord that made him know that he would be king in God's time.

Perseverance

> Remember the earlier days after you had received the light, when you stood your ground in a great contest in the face of suffering. Sometimes you were publicly exposed to insult and persecution; at other times you stood side by side with those who were so treated. You sympathized with those in prison and joyfully accepted the confiscation of your property, because you knew that you yourselves had better and lasting possessions. So do not throw away your confidence; it will be richly rewarded. You need to persevere so that when you have done the will of God, you will receive what he has promised. (Hebrews 10: 32–36)

Persevere: persist, endure, continue, carry on, keep on, keep at it, keep up the good work, stick with it, hold on, stick to one's guns, never say die, stick it out, go through, carry through, follow through, see it through, be diligent, persistent, steadfast, tenacious, constant, unwavering, unrelenting, untiring, patient.

My earliest memories of my dad are of his work. Through much of my life, he was a small business owner. This brought great blessings as well as great challenges. I saw my dad take the good with the bad and keep trudging right along. As his oldest son, I was a part of the business. I was the part that rode in his truck when I was too young to drive, the one who went into the places too small for others, and as I grew, the one who stood up to the task of the hardest job until it was completed. Some of my most treasured memories and my most difficult life experiences occurred while working in the family business.

My dad was an amazing man. He was one of the smartest self-taught men I have ever known and, in his prime, could work twice as hard and long as anyone else on the job. Even after getting on in years, he could stay with a job longer than men half his age. As I

62

tenacity, and courage were required. Moses had to faithfully endure the trials of Pharaoh so that he could endure the testing of his own people.

After numerous confrontations with Pharaoh and many incredible manifestations of God's provision and power, the people were delivered from slavery. However, because of their lack of confidence in their God, a two-week stroll to the promised land became a forty-year test of endurance and perseverance. Israel's stubbornness and rebellion led to a whole generation dying without attaining the promise. Even Moses had his limits. After years of obedient leadership, he blew it in a weak moment. The results of his disobedience kept him from crossing into the promised land. The closest he came was when God took him to the top of Mount Pisgah to show him the land of promise before he died. One of the most somber passages in the scripture is Deuteronomy 34:5, "*Moses the servant of the Lord died in the land of Moab.*"

After Moses, Joshua led Israel into the land of promise. He defeated the inhabitants, destroyed their strongholds, and divided the land among the tribes of Israel. Joshua lived out his days in the company of people like Caleb who believed God. Near the end of his days, Joshua declared to the people, "*Chose you this day whom you will serve, whether the gods which your fathers served that were on the other side of the river, or the gods of the Amorites in whose land you dwell. But as for me and my house, we will serve the Lord.*" Unfortunately, after the "Joshua Generation" died out, Israel forgot the Lord. They did not persevere.

After Joshua, Israel slipped further and further from the best that God had promised. They forgot the covenant of the Lord and found themselves living under the curse of disobedience, idolatry, and rebellion. They were harassed and mistreated by the very people that they had displaced. Others like the Philistines rose to power and subdued Israel. Though they were no longer living as slaves in Egypt, they lived in fear and depravation. They were weak, and their enemies were strong. Israel lived in this manner for nearly four hundred years.

Through the course of nearly four centuries, God anointed judges to arise from among the people to lead them to victory against their enemies. Seven distinct times God brought deliverance and the opportunity for Israel to return to pure worship and covenant relationship. Seven distinct times Israel set aside God's law and substituted it with, *"Everyone did what was right in his own eyes"* (Judges 21:25.) Although time after time, God's amazing power was manifest on behalf of his people, Israel demonstrated an inability and unwillingness to consistently follow him. The history of Israel is a repetitive cycle of rebellion, chastisement, and redemption. Over and over, we see the contrast between the faithfulness of God and the unfaithfulness of his chosen people.

It is not as if faithfulness is unattainable. As a young boy, David proved to be a faithful shepherd with a heart for God. His willingness to persevere in spite of life's obstacles made him a giant slayer. David became a successful leader because of his desire to honor God. He became a hero, a deliverer, and a wealth-building king. Under David's leadership, Israel was united as never before. The nation returned to God and experienced a revival of covenant relationship. David was a man after God's own heart.

Lest one think that David lived a charmed life, it is important to note: he experienced frequent attack, unfair hardship, unjust accusation, rejection by his wife, treachery of friends, rebellion of a son, and the darkness of his own heart. David suffered because of bad choices. The consequences of his sin had their effect. Yet when David was confronted with his sin, he never failed to acknowledge it, repent, and seek God's forgiveness. Ultimately, this allowed David to persevere.

To follow every example is not necessary for the purpose of this book. But think of kings like Asa, Jehoshaphat, and Hezekiah, or prophets like Isaiah, Jeremiah, and Daniel. These and others were simply men who were given the exceptional opportunity to honor God with their lives. They were not perfect, but they were persistent. That's why they are excellent examples for us.

You need to persevere so that when you have done the will of God, you will receive what he has promised. You will be tested in your perseverance! As I wrote the pages of this book, my resolve was tested over and again. Church problems will always be with us. Interpersonal conflict, misunderstandings, opinionated people, inconsistent Christians, and fair-weather friends are easy to be found. Never forget, we are seldom blindsided by the big issues of life. They are easy to see coming, and the saints usually rally together in the face of major obstacles. It is *the little foxes that spoil the vine.* Those things that seem to be insignificant to most have a way of accumulating. In fact, to ask for help or to voice concern regarding the *little foxes* might seem petty to the average person. Because of this, most of us never mention these little things. Yet the little things very often do the most damage because we are helpless to stop them. Don't waste time trying to stop something that you cannot control. Don't spend time complaining, stewing, or seething over these issues. File them where they belong. Put them under the blood. There are things that you cannot handle on your own, but there will never be anything that Jesus cannot handle.

Be determined to do the right thing! Persevere: persist, endure, and continue: Persistence is a word that few today understand. If things get hard, quit! If you might lose money, bail! If the relationship gets rocky, divorce! If problems arise, leave. After all, it's what everybody else does. Knock off early, stay home and rest, give up, give in, give out, and throw in the towel. This attitude has crept into our vocations, our families, and our churches. If problems arise, just quit! This response is foreign to the minds of previous generations, and foreign to the word of God.

"You need to persevere so that when you have done the will of God, you will receive what he has promised" (Hebrews 10:36 NIV).

Perseverance is the key to success in any venture. Especially in the church. Pastors above all should develop a tenacious work ethic. Remember earlier, I wrote, "Some of my most treasured memories and my most difficult life experiences came from working in the family construction company." It was those times, good and bad, that prepared me for the work of my life.

As a pastor, I have encountered great joy and blessing right along with great grief and frustration. Long hours, endless meetings, unresponsive, unappreciative, mean-spirited leaders, spiritually dead complainers, etc., all take their toll on a pastor. There is an accumulative effect that can grow into a weight that is not easy to bear. Unfortunately, good times do not get the same amount of press as the bad. Happy events are not imprinted as strongly in our minds as unhappy experiences are. The reason for this is that bad things are just not supposed to happen. When they do, they stand out. Our society has conditioned us to expect "good things" to be the norm. We enjoy them when they come, but few people are careful to note them as significant events. The idea that we should never have problems is not supported by scripture. "*It rains on the just and on the unjust.*" David, in Psalm 22, cried out, "*My God, My God, why have you forsaken me? And why are you so far from the voice of my cry?*"

Scripture teaches that we have a companion that sticks closer than a brother. He accompanies us into life's valleys, walks with us through the storms of life, and enjoys the good things that we encounter. I believe that it is only our Americanized version of Christianity that convinces us that bad things only happen to bad people. Satan loves to get us off track by having us looking for hidden sin or for someone on whom we can blame our misfortune. Because of this, we very often fail to recognize the companionship we have with Jesus. At times, it is the harshness of life that exposes the tenderness of our Father. His strength, protection, and supply become clearer in the light of our greatest needs. Yet in our times of need, frustration and complaint rise from our lips like smoke from a fire.

What a mess! We miss the point of "*give thanks in all things.*" "*Count it all joy when…*" sends us into a tailspin. "Brother! You just don't know how hard it is!" "Nobody knows the trouble I've seen. Nobody knows my suffering." Pastors struggle with hurt feelings, rejection, frustration, and other stressors. Burnout has become as frequent as blessing in many pastorates. If anyone tells you differently, he is either lying on a temporary honeymoon, uninformed, or brain damaged. Problems come. Misunderstandings arise. Balance is hard to maintain. Just when you get everything set, somebody throws their stuff on the pile, usually at five o'clock on Friday or right before the service on Sunday morning.

What if I pastor the devil's dream team?

Nehemiah had Sanballat, Tobiah, and Geshem the Arab. Job had Elophaz, Bildad, and Zophar. Daniel had the jealous governors and satraps conspiring against him. Paul had Alexander the Coppersmith. Jesus had his Judas. You don't need to think that you will avoid your own adversaries. I'm sure every pastor will at least be tested and at worst be bested by those whose goal in life is to have their own way and hurt the man of God. They care little for the long-term effects of their words and actions. All they want is to get their way. They must be in control! Although their methods may differ slightly, they are driven by disruptive and destructive spirits. Some may not initially realize their actions are poison to the work of God. Nevertheless, the fact that they yield so completely to the carnal nature indicates they either were never born again or they are backslidden in their faith. A man or woman with a fresh, spirit-filled relationship with the Father cannot consistently act in ways contrary to the word and purpose of God.

At times, we will liken these disrupters to biblical characters that had ill motives. They may be like at least two of David's sons. The first born, Amnon, became obsessed with his half-sister, Tamar. He went to great lengths to get her alone so that he could let her know his intent. When Tamar refused to lie with him, he forced himself upon her and immediately his desire for her turned to hatred. The darkness of his heart began a course of destruction that he could have never imagined. "*Then, when desire has conceived, it gives birth to sin; and sin, when it is full-grown, brings forth death*" (James 1:15 NKJV). Amnon never imagined that his selfish desire would ultimately cost him his life and the lives of others. Yet this scenario has played out a myriad of times through history. We can easily find the same result in the ruins of countless churches and communities today.

Absalom, the third son of David, was a patient schemer who took two full years to plan and exact vengeance upon his older brother, Amnon. Absalom was not overtaken by passion as Amnon had been. He was overtaken by anger and offense. He justified his scheming by considering his sister's shame. He was sure that his father, David, had known what had happened to his sister but did nothing. So Absalom's vengeance grew to encompass any and everyone who could have or should have intervened.

Absalom's determined vengeance for his sister was well planned and executed. The problem was, his anger had grown far beyond Amnon. Absalom's plan to kill his brother grew into a plan to displace his father and take over the kingdom. The troubles caused by a vengeful heart interrupted the plan of God, put the kingdom of Israel in jeopardy, caused the death of many, and ultimately, cost Absalom his life. Today we know the "Absalom spirit" as one whose attempt to lead includes scheming to remove legitimate leaders.

When an Absalom spirit settles into a heart of a man or woman, they justify their actions based on some past offense that no one else remembers. Their focus narrows until their only desire is to have their way. The damage that follows simply becomes a necessary consequence. After all, the blame is upon whoever failed to do whatever they thought should have been done in any given situation. What likely could have been addressed with understanding, forgiveness, and godly principle is now being handled with outright rebellion. There is complete disregard for the damage and pain cause to others. In the church, the Absalom spirit usually settles upon someone with leadership responsibilities. Staff members, deacons, or other influencers within the church can develop heart of an Absalom. In his day, Absalom quietly gained the confidence of the people by whispering about the king. "If I were in charge, this is how I would do it..." The constant drip of criticism and suggestion eventually has it effect.

In Absalom's defense, if there is any, we would do well to remember the other actors in the story. Amnon was the first culprit in the story. He intentionally manipulated his own sister into a position of pain and shame. Amnon's lustful obsession created the whole sorted mess. But then there was David, the man after God's own heart. He may have been the greatest king, the most celebrated hero, and most popular psalmist, but he was a pitiful dad. There was no apparent comfort for a broken daughter. There was no correction for an evil son. And after Absalom killed Amnon, David refused to even see his son Absalom for over five years. The accumulation of tragedy without remedy created the man that Absalom became. The lesson here is that we should be forthright in examining and dealing with the issues we face. When we ignore a matter rather than address it, it grows larger with time.

There is another biblical character we recognize that led God's people astray, displaced righteousness, and introduced her own brand of control upon the people of Israel. Ahab married the daughter of Ethbaal, the king of the Sidonians. Her name, Jezebel, literally meant, "Where is the prince?" which was a ritualistic question shouted in ceremonies honoring Baal. While we might think that would give him pause, Ahab ran with it. He stood back as Jezebel took control of the kingdom, killed the prophets of God, and imported her own prophets to impose the worship of Baal and Asherah on a national scale.

Jezebel is cunning and loves control. She often works subtly with whispers and suggestions that plant doubt in the hearts of her victims. Her goal is to usurp authority and assume control for herself. Jezebel does not care who she hurts along the way. She builds strong-holds in the hearts of people, presents a religious image, and entices people away from the truth. Jezebel hates the prophetic and rebels against biblical authority. If Jezebel can, she will develop a follow-ing by appealing to the pride in people's lives. Jezebel hates genuine repentance, opposes righteousness, and craves control. Witchcraft is her gift, and her ultimate desire is to place herself on the throne.

The original Jezebel was the wife of King Ahab. However, the "Jezebel spirit" can and does rest upon men or women. Until Jezebel has been exposed, you may think that person is your best friend and supporter. Yet Jezebel must have his or her way. Say "no" to their plans, and it will seem like all hell is coming against you. Division, distraction, intrusion upon the plan of God, and outright attack is the goal. Generally, the destruction is significant, and the casualties are numerous because Jezebel is seldom exposed until the ground-work has been laid.

There are some common characteristics that may help iden-tify the spirit of Jezebel in an individual. First among these is that the individual in question will never admit guilt or being wrong.

They always deflect responsibility. There is never a genuine apology or evident repentance because there was "never" anything wrong. Any admission will turn the issue back toward the authority figure. "I'm sorry you misunderstood." "What I said may have been above your head." "I'm sorry you took it that way. You must be sensitive." "Your misinterpretation is what caused the confusion." Jezebel is all about self and will use people without pause. Jezebel uses manipulation through flattery, well-placed suggestions, or subtle suggestions. She will pull the strings and cause others to do the dirty work. The Jezebel spirit is so masterful the individual under her influence will believe the idea for action came from their own heart. All the while, Jezebel will sit quietly in the background, looking very innocent. Anytime you directly confront Jezebel, there is immediate denial and defensiveness. The issue at hand will be so completely turned around on you, you may walk away feeling you had imagined it all. Jezebel always pretends to know more than is told. You will walk away from your conversation with the nagging feeling that you don't have the complete picture. In Jezebel's world, information is power. That information is used to stir emotion and keep you off balance and troubled. You will also realize that the person is a master at fishing for information.

In Jezebel's day, Ahab was a weak-willed king who relinquished the power of the throne to a godless wife. She killed the prophets, murdered to please her husband, and moved the hearts of Israel from God to pagan idols and deities. She manipulated, distorted, controlled, and brought great damage to everyone she touched. The spirit/character of Jezebel is alive and well today.

The character of an Absalom may take the form of the "head deacon or church boss," a trusted staff member, a supposed close friend, or an influential member of the church. The culprit may be a businessman with resources who, because of his relative wealth, his social standing is elevated, and he may have been promoted to leadership without biblical qualifications. He is not held to the same standards that may be imposed upon others simply because of his social standing. The treasurer and others feel the need to report to him, and he feels important.

There may be one or more secondary leaders who are controlled by the first. They gained control over time and feel secure. There are those who love being in control, others love to stir things up. He may have been the schoolyard bully and still likes pushing people's buttons, or he was the school nerd who feels better about himself if he can make others miserable. Either way, this behavior plays right into Absalom's hand. In essence, he becomes the front man for the "church boss." People expect him to act up. "Oh! Don't mind him, that's just the way he is. I'm sure he doesn't mean it the way it sounds. Just rise above it." His job is to deflect attention from the real issues. He throws the church into turmoil or at least provides the pastor with a few sleepless nights. Anytime that Absalom's authority comes into question, the number two becomes a hit man. He is known to be and instigator and agitator. Remember, the Absalom spirit loves to know people's secrets and will use them to manipulate others when it is beneficial. If he doesn't know any secrets, he is happy to make something up!

Finally, there is the one given to the spirit of Jezebel. She is on the same team with the others but doesn't take orders from any-one. She may be a greeter or in some other place of influence in the body. She is subtle and cunning. A Jezebel spirit drives her. Once entrenched, the Jezebel spirit is capable of more damage than those with the Absalom spirit combined. Her work is insidious. Jezebel turned a whole nation from God. If allowed to, Jezzie will turn a whole church. She uses suggestive words subtly and half-truths. She will be the one with the most active phone—Facebook or Instagram ministry.

She will put herself in position as an influencer. She wants to gain the confidence of newcomers as quickly as possible. "Welcome to our church," she might say. "We want to welcome you into our fellowship. We are blessed to have such a move of God and glad you are here to experience God with us." In her midweek telephone call, she is gracious but drops one or two negative tidbits into the conver-sation. "We love our worship. There is so much freedom, but don't you think things would be better if there were more hymns?" "We really have been blessed. The pastor is great, but he sure spends a lot of time on the golf course." By her third contact or so, Jezzie offers negative opinions more freely. The shame is that she looks good on the outside. Eventually, you notice those she has befriended either do not stay or they begin to express the dissatisfaction she has planted. She is like the enemy who sowed the tares among the wheat.

Most of the time, a new pastor will be warned about these individuals. At times, it will be one instigator warning about the others. Most of the church is aware of their behavior, but amazingly, they are allowed to continue unchecked. What is a pastor to do? Pray and be ready to confront these individuals when the time comes. If you act in God's timing instead of your own, you may have to weather a storm or two, but you and your church will survive and be made better for it. Persistence is key.

Your best tools will be the word of God and a consistent, honest character. Always be willing to openly do the right thing no matter the cost and know the Word of God. The constitution and bylaws of our churches are often overlooked; as a result, the unqualified are often elevated to positions of leadership. If you take the time to earn the trust of the congregation and demonstrate character and wisdom, the church will stand when Jezebel and Absalom are confronted. Do not, however, be surprised if there are those who feel sorry for the poor mistreated offenders.

Leaders matter

After salvation by grace, two of the central teachings of my ministry have been, whatever is in the head will find its way into the body, and we must always do the right thing even if it costs us extra. Scripture is clear in the fact that Jesus is the head and that we are the body. Equally clear is that we are expected to become more like him every day. Romans 8 says, we are *predestined to be conformed to the image of His son.* Paul wrote to the early church that we should be imitators of him as he is of Christ. With all this in mind, I believe it is no great leap to assert that what character traits abide in the leader will in some way manifest in those under that leadership. If the head is passionate, caring, committed, loving, and giving, the body will eventually display those characteristics. On the other hand, if the head is dispassionate, corrupt, unethical, and immoral, those traits will eventually become manifest in the body.

This does not occur over night. It takes time. The virtue of patience is as necessary as the willingness to root out ungodly characteristics and habits developed over time. Without doubt, these two principles go hand in hand. The serious pastor will recognize that most Christian characteristics are better caught than taught. They model a Christlike lifestyle before their congregations. They are consistent with their words as well as their actions. Over time, people find sincere Christianity appealing in their pastor.

The persistent pastor who consistently stands strong on behalf of the people eventually builds a congregation who will stand for him in times of need. I'm not promoting neediness among pastors, but issues of life happen to us all. When issues do arise, it is a healthy pastor and church who find themselves standing strong together.

CHAPTER 8

CHANGING CHURCHES

King David's campaign against the Philistines had significantly weakened an old foe. As a result, Israel had taken control of much of the fertile land of the region of Gaza. Jewish settlers and farmers had pushed into the area to the southeast and had established their crops. They had just enjoyed two seasons of uninterrupted harvest for the first time in years. Now they were almost surprised to hear, "They (the Philistines) are coming back." The word of an impending invasion had reached Joab, the commander of David's armies. Joab sent Shammah, one of the three mightiest of all David's men, south to scout the situation. His job was to determine if the threat was real, identify defensive positions, develop initial plans of defense in case it was needed, and organize the local farmers. Joab and the main body of the army was two days away, but according to their scouts, any Philistine attack was four to five days out at the earliest.

The smell of wood smoke was heavy in in the air the night that Shammah arrived in the small village just southeast of the old Philistine town of Gath. They had settled the area in the hope that the Philistines had finally been vanquished. Yet here they were again, waiting for an attack. The people of the village were visibly nervous at hearing the Philistines were gathering their forces. The memories of the past troubled their minds. The potential Philistine rampage would bring great hardship to a people who were trying to start over. If reports were true, the village was in the path of the gathering Philistine army.

Clearly, the people had forgotten the might of David's armies and the stories of victory. After all, Shammah had been one of the leaders who had help to take the land and subdue Israel's enemies. But now he had trouble even getting the villager's attention. Fear was taking over. Panic was settling in. The intimidating spirit of the Philistine army was effective far in advance of their arrival. It was as if the Philistine giant had come back to life and was hurling threats and accusations their way.

Sometimes we choose to remember the wrong details. God's people often remember the struggle more than the victory. In truth, the philistines had been a persistent enemy for generations. No matter how many times they were defeated, they just always seemed to come back. It's the same with the adversary of our day. He is defeated but persists in causing trouble. His goal is to catch us off guard, get us off track, and limit our effectiveness. We are equipped with the appropriate armor. Our weapons are mighty. But there are times when we are weary from the fight. Like the Philistines of old, he just keeps coming back.

Shammah's first morning in the village of Ruel was the same as many other mornings before battle. The busy work of starting the day was compounded by the frantic scrambling of the frightened villagers. Everyone rushed to gather what they could while others seemed to wander aimlessly overwhelmed by the possibilities of attack. The sun had scarcely risen when the other shoe dropped. Not only were the Philistines coming but they were arriving far earlier than initial reports suggested. The Philistines would reach the area near the village of Ruel by nightfall.

Shammah gathered the village elders and the young men to lay out a plan of defense. Only a few of the men of the village had served the king, and most of the elders had only fought for Saul before David. They were rusty, untested, and frightened out of their wits. It was clear that the people of the village were in trouble. No amount of strategizing seemed to help them remember their God as a defender. In the face of an approaching army, these men could only imagine defeat. The approach of the Philistine army was real. Imminent destruction was a forgone conclusion. This was their reality. More than once, Shammah found himself wondering what he was doing in this insignificant little village that had no strategic value. Every time the thought arose, the answer was right there with it. King David had won this land. These were people of Israel; they mattered! Shammah was here to serve his king no matter the cost.

No matter how hopeless this situation was, and no matter how frightened these people were, Shammah had been sent ahead to make preparation for the coming battle. So he formed the settlers and farmers into troops and appointed them strategic positions from which to meet the Philistine army. The women and children were evacuated to the safest place they could find. Anything that could be useful to the approaching army was either hidden well or destroyed.

Shammah's hope was that the enemy would be weary from their march and rest before the attack. Although this was a two-edged sword. Philistines resting in camp gave Joab more time to arrive, but the thought of a rested enemy was troubling. Shammah prayed that Joab and the army would arrive sooner than expected. When the Philistine army came into view, it was almost sundown. They began to make camp. There was one prayer answered!

During the night, many of the villagers faded away into the darkness. They didn't mind calling Ruel their home, but they were not willing to take a stand for it. Their lack of commitment to their own cause and the outright cowardice of the people was breathtaking. In the light of the second morning, Shammah found himself almost standing alone. In fact, there were so few defenders left it took the Philistines a bit to realize there was any resistance at all. That was when they saw Shammah.

Person after person all but begged Shammah to flee the village. After all, if those who lived there thought so little of their home, why should he? "Who are you? Who do you think you are? You are only going to make things worse! This is not your fight. You are going to ruin your calling and career." But Shammah knew who he was! He understood his calling and responsibility. He knew that he could have run, but then he would have to face himself afterward. It simply was not in him to run. He did not hide from the enemy but embraced his calling as one of the mightiest of King David's mighty men. Shammah stood his ground, ready to defend Ruel with his last breath. He took his position on the outskirts of the village, facing the Philistine encampment. He stood his ground in the middle of a field of lentils, and as he did so, the remainder of Ruel's brave defenders melted away. What looked like Shammah's last stand was a pea patch!

Shammah began to fight and just kept standing his ground and killing Philistines as long as they kept coming. The Lord had found a man that he could work through. The willing hands and faithful heart of Shammah in that pea patch on the outskirts of an unknown village wrought an unbelievable victory. Of this story, the scripture says that "the Lord brought about a great victory." It is important to understand that it may have been Shammah's stand but it was the Lord's victory. Remember who you are in him and who sent you to fight.

Changing churches

Is changing churches intriguing? Most of us are looking for that perfect church. We're looking for a place where we can minister freely to people who love God, love his Word, and love one another. Many churches are looking for the perfect pastor who meets their needs, is not overly concerned with himself or his family, and has a lot of faith. Generally, the first year of most pastorates go smoothly. Everyone is on their best behavior. After all, it is the honeymoon period, and besides, most pastors leave after eighteen to twenty-four months anyway. So don't sweat it. The problem with this logic is that successful churches and ministries are those who develop a long-term vision and walk it out with diligence. Rebuilding a leadership team ever two years or so may promote the honeymoon stage but does little to develop the church. Every once in a while, there comes a pastor who knows God's call to a specific church. He has vision that causes him to look beyond the short term. He has learned that a long-term relationship between the pastor and the church is vital. In addition, this pastor realizes the intense need to find and live as close as he can to the perfect will of God. He has learned some hard lessons that impressed upon him the necessity of standing when everyone else said run. Such a pastor will make a determined stand upon the integrity of the Word of God. He will at times face opposition. There will be power struggles. Traditions will need to be broken. Perhaps transition will be easy. But very likely not.

God is true to his word. He really is a rewarder of those who diligently seek him. He never offers vision as a tease. Vision reveals possibilities and gives direction. But take care and be determined. Even God doesn't always get his way. You won't either unless you are willing to become a modern-day Shammah and defend your pea patch as everyone around you flees.

The church I pastor was founded in 1921 and is one of the oldest Assemblies of God churches in our state. We still have decedents of founding members in the body. During its history, this church has produced a number of preachers who went on to become successful pastors. One North Texas District superintendent was saved and called to the ministry during a revival in our church. There were times that this church was a "flagship church" in our state.

As far as I have been able to tell from study of old business-meeting minutes, word of mouth of former pastors, and the verbal history shared by congregants, this church fell into a long season of inward struggle in the early to mid-seventies. Power struggles and church politics forced two long-term pastors to resign after serving sixteen years each. Both instances resulted in church splits and new congregations in the community. That really doesn't help the identity of a church in a small community.

By the time I came on the scene, a couple of the deacons had decided that seven years was long enough for any pastor to stay in *their* church. They made it their mission to see that time limit established. After all, they had lived through the ouster of two long-term pastors and knew the damage of a beloved pastor being forced out. Somehow, they saw congregational love and support for the pastor as a problem. Their own actions and behavior were never considered as a contribution to church problems. There was a built-in opposition to and disrespect for pastoral leadership that had been entrenched for generations. When we arrived, we faced resistance to anything that could break the negativity. Gossips abounded, disunity and disharmony were the norm, and Jezebel was in the house. All the while, the average member had no clue as to the behind the scenes struggle of the pastor.

In my first year, the youth pastor's car tires were slashed by members of the youth group during a service, and the board refused to help him with the expense. During my second year, one deacon made it his habit to provide me with a written critique of my sermons, visitation schedule, personal integrity, or whatever else he could dream up. Another deacon consistently spread the word that we were failing financially and would soon have to fire our custodian of thirty-plus years. Completely untrue, but damaging nonetheless. Subtle suggestions, careful accusations, and persistent slanderous statements emanated from the very men who were chosen to assist and support the pastor. Board meetings became so volatile I openly placed a tape recorder on the board table in the hope that its presence would curtail the vicious attacks that had become so common.

In all honesty, I was miserable. Yet I knew that God had directed my wife and I to this church. Even so, I tried to renegotiate our assignment more than once. Thankfully, our children were young adults and did not require as much attention as in earlier years. So we were able to pour ourselves into the call. At times, there seemed to be opposition on every side. Resources were frozen. Any outreach had to demonstrate a direct dollar return. Leader's behavior continually pushed people away. Numbers fell. Finances fell. The bottom-line thinkers became agitated. The only thing I knew for sure was that God had brought me to our church and would not talk to me about leaving. So I dug in. I prayed, preached the Word, and loved God's people. Four years into the pastorate after one especially difficult board meeting, the Lord released me to directly confront the inappropriate behavior of several of the deacons. I had been prayerful, patient, and the congregation by now knew my heart. Besides, I was quite tired of the abuse. It was time! When the dust settled, four of the seven deacons agreed to sign an agreement to conduct themselves in agreement with the scriptures and our constitution and bylaws.

Three did not. A twenty-three-year deacon, a twelve-year deacon, and a three-year deacon refused.

Three days after confronting the offending members of the board, three men simply resigned their position with the threat of leaving the church with about fifty of their closest friends and a huge amount of financial support. The other four deacons adopted a statement of responsibility and entered into the minutes that succeeding boards were to review a document on pastor-board relations on an annual basis and sign a commitment form, stating their willingness to honor God with their behavior as leaders in the church. We also proposed and passed a bylaw change that provided for a rotating deacon system. With that, we were on the road to unity between the board and the pastor. It had cost people and finances we could ill afford to lose, but the right thing is the right thing no matter the cost.

In the days following, it seemed everywhere my wife and I turned, we were confronted with accusations. "I heard you threatened to hit a deacon." "I heard you forced the deacons to sign the church property over to you." "I heard…" "I heard…" The stress almost broke us; we couldn't even go to the local grocery store without being assaulted with these accusations. Broken, discouraged, and depressed, we retreated to the church sanctuary. All either of us wanted was to find a little comfort and peace. Our hope was to lay upon the altar and not be faced with the continued injustice. Instead of the gentle comforting voice of the Father, I received a bit of a rebuke. "Who do you think you are? Get up! Quit your crying. Defend your calling, guard this church, and continue your stand."

At that moment, he reminded me again that this was not a natural struggle. The problems we faced were not about me! It was a spiritual stronghold that had to be broken. So right there we began to take authority in the name of Jesus. We rebuked every demonic spirit we could name and probably made up a few. It might seem foolish today, but I found myself walking barefoot across the pews and over sections of the sanctuary, taking back territory. Our demeanor changed. Our confidence returned, and we turned a distinct corner in the life of our church. It is good to know whose you are and who you serve.

I have always believed that whatever was in the head would in time be manifest in the body. The change in the makeup of the board of deacons allowed for unity among leadership to grow. Our newfound unity established the pattern for the congregation. In no time, our people began to recognize a sense of unity and harmony among church members. People began to linger after services so they could visit. Gossip quickly began to diminish, and genuine relationships began to develop. *"Behold, how good and how pleasant it is for brethren to dwell together in unity!"* (Psalms 133:1 NKJV).

Since this is no fairy tale, I won't suggest that everything was suddenly perfect. I will say that we were given a chance. I still had the great responsibility of pastoring in a positive and encouraging fashion. I had to consistently declare the blessing and favor of the Lord over our church. We still had a few naysayers shouting from outside the congregation. Our people occasionally needed to be reminded to be careful what or who they listened to, and I learned to drag the darkness into the light. The more we testified about God's favor and the more we exposed the darkness, the stronger we grew.

I have found it important to never allow malicious behavior the comfort of darkness. When slander and gossip arose, I simply and quickly brought it before the body. I never lashed out, did not speak in anger, but simply told the truth in love. I reminded our people of the love of God, the progress we had made, the vision he had given us, and our need to protect the unity God had given. It worked. I have become convinced that whisperers lose their impact when their dishonesty is exposed. Soon I found myself referring to the "new board." In fact, twenty years later, I still find myself speaking that phrase. The focus of our board meetings changed. We grew from being "bottom-line thinkers" to being kingdom thinkers. Sometime around year seven, the board and I began making big plans for a major and long-past due renovation of our sanctuary. We all felt the finances would come in to support the plan. So with great enthusiasm, we began implementing our plans. Then for no apparent reason, the next month's general fund receipts dropped by $4,000.00.

Dread filled my heart, and I absolutely hated the thought of meeting with the board. The past had conditioned me to expect the worst when the finances plummeted. Now the positive visionary pastor of last month had to face the deacons. Their immediate response was, "It's just a test! We're with you, Pastor. No need to stop now." What a difference! Our long-overdue renovation turned out to be a major victory. The work went well. The upgrades enhanced our facility's appearance, functionality, and comfort. Even the naysayers were blessed by the change. Over the course of ten months, more than one hundred thousand dollars came in above tithes and offerings. During the project, our general fund receipts increased by nearly 20 percent. That was quite an accomplishment, considering where we had been. We went from outdated to modern-looking, and the result was growth. Our members became more confident. Our guests came and stayed.

Since that time, we have consistently grown in our local ministries, outreach, missions support, and resources. Our people continue to grow in the love of God and love for one another. He has given us a great degree of favor and prominence in our community. Our board, staff pastors, volunteer pastors, and members are embracing the vision of reaching our city more strongly than ever. In the years prior to the COVID-19 pandemic, we had more than two hundred people a year embrace Jesus as their Savior in regular Sunday services. Very quickly, our newly renovated sanctuary was no longer large enough. Today I am enjoying pastoring more than any other time in my ministry. I believe we have more potential than ever.

While all the struggles mentioned were going on, the church was a relatively strong and looked good from the outside. Outward appearances are greatly deceiving. In truth, the church will never grow beyond leadership struggles whether the people are aware or not. The health and strength of the church is not found in the bottom line but in the way it stands before the Lord. This brings to the fore the necessity for God to change his church. He desires the church to be spotless and without blemish. Clearly then, the church must become different than we find it in most places. Since the Father chooses to work through his people, it is necessary for the faithful to take a stand upon the principles of the word on behalf of the church. That is where we come in.

In the church world, there is very little greener grass. When you see lush green fields, you will usually find that the church has been carefully nurtured by a senior pastor and leadership team who at some point learned that instead of changing churches, they should look to God to bring change to the one he serves.

CHAPTER 9

ONCE YOU GET IT FIXED

David, king of Israel, was a man of grand gestures and great exploits. He was blessed and favored by God and ultimately succeeded in all that he did as a king. David was heroic and passionate. When he was turned toward the Lord, he was a man to admire. When he was in himself, like all of us, his decisions were disappointing.

The men who gathered with him were inspired by his courage and cunning. Thirty or so of them had been with him since the early days in the Cave of Adullam. They were a part of the broke, busted, and disgusted crowd that had fled from King Saul. The very people who were broken by Saul grew under David. They fought by his side against the enemies of Israel and stood by him as they were all pursued by Saul. Some became known as men of valor. They were the ones who arrived early and stayed late. These were men who fought beyond what was expected. They fought for the outcome. Their families depended on it. Their young king needed them to succeed. Their God saw their hearts and granted the strength and anointing to stand up to the task. They stood their ground until they won. These were men who started well and ended well. They were inspired by David's courage, character, and heroics. In many cases, their exploits exceeded those of David. After all, they were the defenders of the giant slayer.

There were men like the one called Adino (sharp and strong) whose real name was Josheb-Basshebeth, who killed eight hundred men in one battle. Eleazar who stood with David against the Philistines when the rest of Israel's army retreated, and then there was Shammah. Shammah was the man who refused to run when everyone around him fled. He stood his ground in the middle of a pea patch and fought until the enemy had been defeated. Their courage and valor won battles, established a nation, and inspired younger men to follow their example.

The sons of these men were inspired by their dads and mentors. They pushed back against natural boundaries and became men of valor in their own right. Benaiah was the son of a valiant man from Kabzeel in the southernmost part of the kingdom. Inspired by the example of his dad and other heroes of Israel, Benaiah never ran from a fight that needed to be fought. His own exploits, though not as significant at the top three, were nonetheless impressive.

Benaiah had been sent on his first independent assignment of importance. He had been dispatched as an emissary to the king of Moab. His responsibility was to convince the king of Moab of the foolishness of conflict with Israel. Though young and inexperienced, Benaiah had been trained well for the responsibility. He understood that this trip would serve as a benchmark for his future service. He was determined to succeed in his mission.

The Moabite king did not respond well to the young man that David had sent. In fact, he was offended that Israel would send such a young man to meet with him. It was an insult that could not go unanswered. The Moabite king decided to teach David a lesson. He called upon two of his champions to exact retribution upon young Benaiah. In doing so, he would demonstrate to David that he was a man to be respected if not feared.

Benaiah found himself facing two of the mightiest warriors of Moab. They walked in with an air of confidence that spoke for itself. These men had never been beaten. Well paired and seasoned in the art of war, they stepped apart a bit so that they could increase their angle of attack. Benaiah realized that he was in for a fight. He also had to agree with what he had heard of these two. They were impressive! Lionlike is what they had been called. And now they stalked him. Strangely, he was not afraid as they approached.

The two began their attack with slander and ridicule. The Moabites said something about King David's lineage being traced back to a woman of questionable virtue. Clearly, they were trying to get inside his head. When their slander turned toward King David, something welled up inside Benaiah. It was not rage or anger; indignation better described what he felt. The Moabites approached with an arrogance that never imagined defeat. They had always won. Everyone they had faced were either killed in battle, died later from their wounds, or fled in terror. Even though there was something different about this young man, they were sure it would be an easy fight. After all, they were standing before their king, surrounded by the officers of his court.

Benaiah ducked under the attack and struck the first blow. His sword bit deep into the forearm of the largest. His friend attempted to strike, but Benaiah was too fast. He parried the blow and allowed his sword to slide smoothly through the man's defense and ended his fight right there. The first had regrouped and realized that he was fighting for his own life. His arrogance faded into the understanding of how his victims had felt before their end. It did not take long. Benaiah's long days of training and instruction from his dad paid off, and he easily defeated these men who so many had feared. Clearly, even lions can be killed.

When Benaiah turned from the battle to face the King of Moab that day, the whole atmosphere had changed. No longer did he appear so young in the king's eyes. The king's offense quickly faded, and Benaiah left with the full assurance of the king that no further incursions into Israel would be sanctioned. Benaiah was no longer in the shadow of his dad. He had learned to cast his own.

Once you and I get the bad habits and dysfunction of yesterday behind us, we get to relax! After all, it has been an intense fight that was far more than a battle. We just walked through a spiritual war with the help of the Lord. The intensity required increased our focus in our prayer. We walked with extreme diligence as we watched for the attacks of the enemy. At every turn, there was attack, confusion, and accusation. The demand required a level of hypervigilance that was completely exhausting. We deserve a break. We can drop our guard. We can relax. Right? Wrong! After prolonged struggle, we tend to drop our guard. The battle is over, and the Lord has established vindication. Now we can get to the business of building the church. We can begin to grow without people confusing and misleading the saints. We can finally reach our community without the hinderance of old issues and roadblocks. It is a good day.

The truth is that the scripture instructs us to be sober and vigilant because our adversary is constantly on the prowl, looking for whoever he can devour. The adversary's job is to accuse and slander. He loves to steal our resources, kill the work of the Lord, and destroy our lives and ministries. It is his nature. We would always do well to remember that yesterday's victory in no way guarantees that there are no battles to come.

When the shepherd watches the flock, he is responsible for leading them to good grazing and water. He is also responsible for their protection. Predators exist and are driven by their inborn nature to kill. They are competing for their own nourishment. At times, predators get caught up in the excitement and kill because they love the rush. Shepherds lived among the sheep so that predators would sense their presence. At times, they had to stand their ground as wolves, and lions, and bears attacked the sheep. Armed with their staff and sling, the faithful shepherd would defend and rescue the flock in times of danger. Yesterday's peace did not indicate that they could go unarmed. The staff, the sling, and a pouch full of stones were necessary for their profession, so was an alert and watchful eye.

At the risk of over emphasizing the point, I would advise attending to the flock with diligence and plenty of stones in your bag. Predators watch for opportunity. They are cautious and patient. So is our adversary. His tactics seldom change, and his hatred for the Lord's church is constant. His attacks may be delayed, but they are certain. The direction from which the attack comes often vary. One thing is sure, the enemy will use whispers, distortion, subtle suggestions, and outright slander. He is persistent, cunning, and literally out *to steal, kill, and destroy.* He will use the unsuspecting as well as recruits who knowingly carry out his plan. *"For false christs and false prophets will rise and show signs and wonders to deceive, if possible, even the elect* (Mark 13:22). Believers are generally a trusting group. That is why it is possible or even likely that they could be deceived. Scripture says, "*To the pure, all things are pure.*" I take this to mean that we look at the world through redeemed eyes. We have been changed, and at times, we are caught expecting others to have been changed or at least honor the change in us.

A necessary component of the leader's defense of the church is clearly communicated vision. Vision in the sense of direction from the Lord provides clear purpose for the work. Vision defines why and what we do; mission defines the how. The enemy of vision is assumption. When we assume that believers understand the vison simply because they heard it read once or saw it on a banner, we are placing the mission of the church in jeopardy. Vision must be rehearsed to stay fresh. Every new person who attends will bring with them their own experiences and understanding of the church. If the leadership fails to clearly identify vision and mission, the people are left to define it themselves. The result will be, "This is an amazing church. I love everything about it. Why don't we change it!" It may be the worship style or service length. It may be service times or small groups. It may be the emphasis on spiritual depth or lack thereof. The proposed change may even be a decreased focus on reaching the unchurched. The point is that the perfect church will never be made more perfect by conforming to the whims of random attenders. The church is made perfect when it clearly and decisively follows the vision of the Lord for that church.

Every pastor and leader wants their church or ministry to grow. But growth often brings the potential for conflict. Growing pains require a shift. Larger numbers require a difference in pastoral style. The pastoral care in a small rural church will not be the same when that small rural church doubles in size. The very thing that everyone wanted creates tension. "Someone got my seat." "The pastor didn't spend enough time with me." "The new people don't look like us." "The style is different." "The pastor sent his associate for the visit." "The new people are changing things." "I don't know everybody." "I'm not sure I like all of this."

During our Bible college days, my wife, Teri, and I invited some friends to visit the church that we attended. When we came to the sanctuary after Sunday school, our friends were nowhere to be found. We followed up later that afternoon and found that the whole family had accepted our invitation and had come to the church. They arrived early and found a seat in the expansive sanctuary. While they waited, a little lady approached them and said, "You are in my seat. My husband and I always sit here." The lady was so insistent our friends quietly left the church, never to return.

The life and growth of the church is challenged by natural attrition when people pass away, move away, or change churches. The church is attacked by those who would challenge its purpose. The church is at times attacked by the very people who had been attracted to it with intentional effort. At times, it seems that the church is attacked by unethical shepherds of neighboring congregations. Problems arise carelessly and intentionally. Regardless of how they arise, people are often hurt, and progress is stifled.

We are not attending our grandparents' church! Oh, they may have been a part of the same body in years past, but it is not the same. Our churches and ministries have been impacted by the dramatic shifts in society. Some years ago, church-growth experts began to define faithful differently than they had in the past. The standard of faithfulness shifted to describe people who supported the church and attended at least two Sundays a month. That means that if you pastor a church of four hundred, you will see about two hundred on Sunday. We all realized that there had been a shift. Travel, sports, and other activities became a competitor for the church's time slot. The church was left with the option of dying or changing. Adamantly, traditional churches began a rapid downward descent. According to recent research, between 2010 and 2020, church closures among Protestant congregations ranged from 3,850 to 7,700 each year. These numbers amount to 75 to 150 churches per week. The exact numbers are difficult to pinpoint because of the differences in reporting among various denominations. However, it is suggested that these numbers may triple in the aftermath of the pandemic.

As the gradual decline was becoming the norm, additional social upheaval began to occur that hastened the departure of many. Politics combined with social media set people at odds in the late teens and early twenties. The political division of our nation found its way into our churches. As a result, we lost people—some because they disagreed with our politics, some because we did not make our claim strongly enough. The decade from about 2010 to 2020 brought us increased racial division that impacted the church. As a result, there were riots in the streets across our nation for months and months. Whatever the reason, we lost precious members of our church during that time. The significant racial unrest had significant impact upon the church.

The misuse of social media intruded upon the lives of many and distorted their thinking. The further we walked into 2019, the more people lost their grip on a biblical worldview. In becoming virtually connected, we became less connected in reality. The virtual reality of social media allowed people to do and say things they would have never considered otherwise. Early in 2020, the COVID-19 coronavirus descended upon our world. Churches were closed for varying lengths of time around our nation. The moral voice of our communities was silenced over time. Our churches lost ground, and our communities lost the stabilizing influence of a vocal pastor.

The impact upon the church has been significant. After two years, it seems that only about half of the American church has returned to active service. Virtual church has taken the place of actual church for many. Service times are not as crucial as people can access the service or sermon at their leisure. While the flexibility this offers is amazing, it has been hard to see it as a positive move. There is that pesky passage of scripture in Hebrews. *"And let us consider one another in order to stir up love and good works, 25 not forsaking the assembling of ourselves together, as is the manner of some, but exhorting one another, and so much the more as you see the Day approaching"* (Hebrews 10:24–25 NKJV).

What we have learned is what we have known all along. The church is never complete. The work of the church will be constant. There will always be adjustments because there will always be new members to disciple, old members to remind, and attacks from the enemy to thwart. Over the last hundred years, major shifts in the church coincided with generational shifts. Impactful church conflict was random. However, today major shifts and conflict seems to hit the church about every fifteen days. The pastor and church leader of today must be insightful, well read, aware, nimble, and spirit-filled. He must have the wisdom of Solomon, the patience of Job, the strength of Samson, and the tenacity of John on the Isle of Patmos. Legitimate ministry takes many forms and has grown far beyond traditional Sunday and Wednesday meetings. As much as we long for all our people to gather in house, many may never return. Evangelistic outreach is harder. But communication and connection has never been easier. Online, livestream, social media, text messaging, and phone calls all work together to allow for virtual church activity, involvement, and connection. I just pray that it does not become virtual Christianity. Virtual Christianity would be like Jesus speaking to the scribe who had answered well. *"You are not far from the kingdom of God"* (Mark 12:34 NKJV).

Our response to these major societal shifts should be to do everything that we do with excellence and passion. Every service should count! Our worship gatherings should all be approached like Easter Sunday. Every opportunity to worship as a body should be greatly valued. Every encounter with God's people should be seen as an opportunity. These opportunities are wasted if we are just going through the motions. In-person gatherings are an opportunity to know our family better. We should endeavor to make strong connections, help them to grow in the Lord, engage together in the work, cast, and embrace vision more firmly, and look for way to reach others. That's a lot. Yet the goal for every service should be

- strong connections,
- personal growth and discipleship,
- engagement,
- vision casting, and
- outreach.

There are people within the congregation that are uniquely qualified to perform each of these functions. They simply need to realize their call and potential. They need to know your heart, and they need to be released to do the work.

> Let love be without hypocrisy. Abhor what is evil. Cling to what is good. Be kindly affectionate to one another with brotherly love, in honor giving preference to one another; not lagging in diligence, fervent in spirit, serving the Lord; rejoicing in hope, patient in tribulation, continuing steadfastly in prayer; distributing to the needs of the saints, given to hospitality. (Romans 12:9–13 NKJV)

Pastoring the flock is harder than ever. Defending the scattered sheep is amazingly difficult, if not impossible. Isolated sheep are ripe for the picking where the predators are concerned. However, considering the time people spend on their smartphones, their church should be there. We can offer Christian connection, friendship, and resources. Our encouragement can range from simple memes to blog posts. Our sermons can be streamed, archived, reposted, or turned into a podcast. We can preach, stream, post, and boost. We should use every tool at our disposal to grip people's hearts with the truth of God's Word. Our responsibility is to plant and to water. His is to provide the increase. I hate to think we might miss some of the increase because we were looking for it in our old way.

I had the thought recently that if we could return to the wonder and awe that we felt in the early days of our Christian experience, we might find the key to keeping things fresh for our people. I did not grow up in church, so when I accepted Christ and began attending church, everything was new and exciting. It was fresh. I was thrilled to be a part of something so amazing. Everything from the songs to the prayers to the sermons were new to me, and I could not get enough. I had been transformed from someone who did not like crowds or really care for people outside of my family into someone who craved the activity of the church and loved just being there. How to regain the enthusiasm and wonder of new life in Christ may be the question to be answered.

I also remember the early disappointments that I experienced in the church. There were things that surprised me and caught me off guard. The deacons became angry with the pastor. Individual leaders became territorial. Our first business meeting shook us because everyone had an opinion and were willing to fight for their own position. The effect of this was disappointment. The pastor that had led me to the Lord and the church that had introduced me to new life quickly moved from revival to contention and struggle. The discomfort caused by growth caused the saints to forget who and whose they were. I didn't know Christians could act like that. Thankfully, it was during that time that the Lord moved my family and I to Bible college to begin to prepare for our newfound ministry calling. Had we remained in that church long, there is no doubt that we would have found our own territory or opinions to defend.

Remembering the early days of our Christian lives might establish a baseline by which everything else could be measured. Are we in awe, or do we know it all? Have we developed individual and independent schools of philosophy? Or are we building a church that is walking in relationship with Jesus. Is he the head of the body or just a figurehead that we can point to? Like it or not, I can easily understand people leaving a church where they had limited relationships established and little invested. What I cannot fathom is that people might walk away from their relationship with a loving Savior. I can't wrap my head around the possibility that people could so neglect the God of their salvation they could disregard his church. It is hard to take when people wander away without so much as a nod. But none of this has been a surprise to the Lord. (2 Thessalonians 2:3 NKJV).

Without question, we have all witnessed "the falling away." We know those who were once followers of Christ who wandered away from their faith. We have known others who stormed off in a huff. We have also known those who were enticed away by the passions of life. But I am glad to say that there are still faithful followers of Jesus who are still standing regardless of the storms life brings their way.

In most cases, it is their faith that enables them to stand. *"Therefore, my beloved brethren, be steadfast, immovable, always abounding in the work of the Lord, knowing that your labor is not in vain in the Lord"* (1 Corinthians 15:57 NKJV). Just keep in mind, once you get it fixed, the enemy will look for ways to break it again.

CHAPTER 10

CRISIS

The idea was a good one. The people were onboard and excited. It would be amazing to live in the presence of the Lord God every day. David's first major decision after becoming king of all Israel and moving to Jerusalem was to bring the ark of the covenant into the city. The ark represented the very presence and power of God. The ark was said to contain a golden jar of manna, Aaron's staff that had budded, and the stone tablets of the covenant. Above the ark were the cherubim of the glory, facing each other of either side of the mercy seat. The ark rested in the holy of holies in the tabernacle and had done so until the time of Eli, Hophni, and Phinehas, who had lost the ark to the Philistines.

It had been kept in the household of Obed-Edom in Kirjath-Jearim since it had been returned by the Philistines twenty years earlier. The ark had held little or no importance to Israel during the time of King Saul. But now David was finally king. He desired the presence and power of God in his life and among the people. So David and thirty thousand of the choice men of Israel went to gather the ark and set it in a place of prominence in Jerusalem. The problem was that no one had moved the ark for twenty years. The priests who might have had knowledge of the ark had been killed by King Saul. David, Abinadab, and the thirty thousand were on their way to do a good thing, but they were doing it their way.

The Bible tells us of the enthusiastic worship the people enjoyed that day. Instruments of all kinds rang out in celebration. David had a new ox cart constructed for the occasion. The ark was loaded, and they were on their way. As they approached Nachon's threshing floor, the ox stumbled. Uzzah, one of the sons of Abinadab, put out his hand to steady the ark. It was an instinctive reaction, but the wrong move. No one was to touch the ark and live. The anger of the Lord arose against Uzzah, and God struck him, and he died. David had attempted to usher in the presence of the Lord in a careless manner and cost a good man his life.

The fear of the Lord and anger over Uzzah's sudden death stopped David in his tracks. David became afraid of the Lord and returned the ark to the household of Obed-Edom. During the three months that it was there, the priests learned how the ark was to be transported according to the instructions given to Moses. This time they were ready. The priests were prepared, and everyone realized the significance of what they were doing. They were moving the presence of the Lord into their city. The joy of the people was evident, but none more so than David. God had always been with him. His presence and anointing had been constant in his life, and David knew it. From the sheep in the pasture to the palace in the city, God was there, and now the ark would be as well. In spite of their exuberance, David remembered the cost of his carelessness. David's enthusiasm had cost Uzzah his life, and they almost left the ark with Obed-Edom. He had learned a lesson about the danger of doing things his way.

Crisis

The church that Jesus came to build was born in crisis. The Jewish people were living under the harsh rule of the Roman Empire. The religious leaders of his day had significant power and influence over the people. They held a tight grip on their positions and knew how to play Rome's games to survive. The original intentions of the religious leaders of Israel may have been to promote the survival of God's people and their temple worship. However, their compromise created a system that barely resembled God's intention for his people.

Self-preservation became the driving force. A blend of tradition and politics became the norm. So when their promised Messiah arrived, very few recognized or accepted who he was. Jesus was rejected by his own. He was arrested, tried, and crucified for the crime of seeking to save Israel from their sin.

The resurrection of Jesus after his cruel death on the cross was the greatest crisis abatement event in all of history. The moment the disciples saw Jesus standing and alive after his death, their faith was restored, the light came on, and they finally understood what he had taught them from the beginning. He was the Lamb of God sent to take the sin of the world. Without the shedding of blood, there could be no remission of sin, and he had become that perfect sacrifice. The life and death of Jesus had become hope instead of despair. The church was almost ready for its launch. Their final instructions before Jesus ascended to heaven had been to wait. Specifically, wait for the promise of the Father. So that is what they did. The apostles and other followers of Jesus spent days in an upper room in Jerusalem, praying and waiting for that promise. When it came, nothing could hold them back. They were spirit-filled disciples of the resurrected Christ. What could go wrong.

Well, a lot! The day of Pentecost, Peter preached to the crowd that had gathered, and three thousand people received his word and were baptized. When Peter and John encountered the lame man at the gate of the temple, his healing gathered a crowd. So Peter and John preached Jesus to the people in the temple, and five thousand became believers. Unfortunately, not everyone appreciated their enthusiasm. The priest of the temple, the Sadducees, and the temple guard arrested Peter and John and held them in custody overnight. The next day, the two former fishermen found themselves before the temple authorities to answer for their actions. The inquisition focused on how and in whose name had they healed. This was just the first of many such encounters for the Christ followers.

The first pastor of the church of Jerusalem had more problems with attrition than we do. Before the church became known as "the church," its members were so persecuted many fled Jerusalem to other places. New Testament accounts indicate that they suffered financially and struggled to meet the needs of the people. Despite the generosity of their members, the church needed help from time to time. At every turn, the early church was confronted with hardship. The Jewish leaders wanted to stop them. The Romans were largely indifferent toward them. Unbelievers were challenged by them. They were falsely accused, experienced division and doctrinal disputes, and had to call the first church counsel together to define acceptable theology and practice. They weathered the storms of favoritism, sin in the body, the misunderstanding of and misuse of spiritual gifts, as well as abuse of the Lords Supper among its members. Friends and co-laborers in the Lord had misunderstandings at times while others were willing to introduce distorted theology. All the while, these believers experienced the amazingly miraculous intervention of the Lord. Multitudes heard and accepted Jesus as their Savior. Men were raised from the dead, people healed by the passing of Peter's shadow over them, prison bars shaken loose by the power of God, and many other miracles occurred. It was clear that they had been with Jesus, and no one could deny the miracles that so many had seen.

As the years of the first century passed, it became popular to "hate on the Christians." Hebrews 11 says that believers were severely mistreated in an effort to have them deny their faith. They were mocked and scourged, chained and imprisoned. Believers were stoned, sawn in two, tempted and killed with the sword. History tells us that Nero Caesar launched a campaign against the church as a distraction from his political mistakes and misdeeds. The church became his scapegoat. Many were killed simply for his entertainment, and the people of Rome enjoyed it with him. All the apostles but John were eventually martyred for the crime of preaching the gospel and building the church. John was exiled to the Isle of Patmos.

It would serve us well to remember that the early church was born in crisis and that the early church grew dramatically through times of crisis. The fact is, the gospel spread across the known world in part because of crisis. As believers fled persecution, their faith travelled with them. The church was not accepted or supported by society. Those in authority consistently attempted to stifle the growth of the church. Social norms, politics, economics, traditions, cultural divisions, and many other conditions pressed against the church. Yet it flourished. Through history, there have been times the church has been pressed and persecuted and has grown. Believers have been martyred, imprisoned, hounded, and threatened from the first century to today, and still, the church stands.

1 Peter 4:12 says that we shouldn't think that it is strange when difficult times come upon us. Yet I think that much of today's church is crisis weary. After a century of relative ease, the American church is facing a bombardment of crisis. Our world and nation have experienced rapid fire crises in recent years. The climate of social and political unrest is more intense than any other time in our lives. Right and wrong has been redefined and have taken sides. "*Woe to those who call evil good, and good evil; Who put darkness for light, and light for darkness; Who put bitter for sweet, and sweet for bitter! Woe to those who are wise in their own eyes, And prudent in their own sight!*" (Isaiah 5:20–21 NKJV). Lines have been drawn, and our people are more divided than ever. Since the people we reach are naturally a part of our world, they bring their political identities into the church with them. Their pet sins and personal preferences visit with them when they come.

At times, pastors may feel like Paul when he heard from the saints at Chloe's house. "The people are divided. Some favor Paul, some prefer Apollos, while others think Peter is the best." Natural man loves debate, confusion, and absolutes all while living in shades of compromise. The spectrum of political though provides plenty of room for believers to forget who we are. Why pastors and church leaders would think our politics would always align when our theology seldom does is beyond me. One reason our people have always been so easily divided is that we take spiritual identity and discipleship for granted. Genuine relationship must be worked at. We assume, because people like our style, they embrace our theology. The trouble is that the next person we reach starts the process over again.

No question, the church certainly should stand up for biblical convictions. We always ought to filter world events through our understanding of Scripture and teach other believers to do the same. Too often, we have left out the "why" of what we believe. The result has been a church without a biblical worldview. Why do we recognize the problem of sin? Why do we believe that all men need Jesus as savior? What is the biblical definition of a believer? What is marriage? Is sexual sin really sin? How should we approach those in authority? Is it important to attend church regularly? Should we tithe, give, and share? The point is that when we leave the answer to these and other questions blank, someone else will provide the answers.

The world in which we live is regressing relationally rather than advancing. This fact should not surprise us or catch us off guard. Paul said, in the last days, perilous times would come, and they have. The sins of man's past are active in our present and welcome in many of our communities. Our advancements in technology provide the illusion of connection without the reality of relationship. People can meet online, become friends, and fall out with one another without ever meeting in person. The socially accepted norms of the day are far removed from where we were just a few years ago. The further we go, the further we are away from God and his plan for our lives. Very little about our society would suggest that the church would prosper. But social upheaval has never been the determining factor for a successful growing church.

In the last eight years, our crisis weary churches have endured social and racial division, the COVID pandemic, political manipulation, the distortion of truth by the media, the rising cost of living, war, the redefinition of every social norm, and the castigation of those who hold conservative Christian values. The effect has been to quiet the church, diminish its numbers, and weaken its stance in our communities. Our people and preachers are tired. Many have withdrawn from the battle. They are waiting for the crisis to be over.

All this, either by design or misfortune, has had the effect of turning people away from the faith, turning them out of church, and diming the light of their salvation so as not to impact others. It is hard not to imagine that we are living close to the end, but every generation through the ages has thought the same. Living near the end may be precisely why the church has always grown during every storm. Leaders of yesteryear taught to live like it is the last day but prepare as if it may be another one hundred years to come. God's

Word reminds us frequently of our ability to trust his strength and provision. It is time once again to take him at his word and live our lives before him as if we are believers. He has not changed nor has his word. What has changed is that we learned to "do church" without him. We have run off in our own strength and enthusiasm, and now we are paying the price. Like Uzzah, we have put our hand carelessly upon the things of God and have experienced death.

It is time to remember who we are in him and begin to take our stand. "*He gives power to the weak, And to those who have no might He increases strength. Even the youths shall faint and be weary, And the young men shall utterly fall, But those who wait on the Lord Shall renew their strength; They shall mount up with wings like eagles, They shall run and not be weary, They shall walk and not faint*" (Isaiah 40:29–31 NKJV). It is time for his church to wait upon him for his anointing and a fresh infilling of his Holy Spirit in our lives. When we do, we will be transformed from being in distress, in debt, and discontent, to becoming "mighty men and women of valor." We are not here by accident. The Lord has anointed and appointed us for such a time as this. He knows the pitfalls, so he provides the power. This is how it has always been! Stand your ground!

The church should stop waiting for the crisis to be over. Troubled times are nothing new. We need to stop acting like it is. As we learn to stand our ground, the presence and power of the Lord in our lives will win the day. We should stop wasting time grieving over those who have fled and recognize those who gathered with us in the difficult day. The runners may come back, but that is not what you will build upon. The people who stood their ground in the middle of trouble are the men and women of valor who will inspire others to stand. They are the warriors worthy of note. Learn to celebrate them. These are the people to build and rebuild upon. It is time for the faithful to stand with the confidence of the apostle Paul on a sinking ship when he said, "*For there stood by me this night an angel of the God to whom I belong and whom I serve, saying, 'Do not be afraid'*" (Acts 27:23–24 NKJV). Paul knew whose he was and whom he served.

They were rugged, daring, and courageous. They could be counted on when things got tense. These warriors often engage in great exploits on behalf of their king. In spite of the battles, regardless of the challenges, they were people who arrived early and stayed late. These men and women of valor consistently take their stand as encouragers and builders of the kingdom. Their support of their leaders and their commitment to the cause is something to admire. We should be grateful for them and remember to celebrate their exploits. Like Shammah in the field of lentils or Eleazar who stood by the king when others fled, our heroes stood their ground in the face of political and social upheaval, the COVID evacuations, and significant financial challenges. These are the men and women who will build his church. We should strive to be grateful for what adversity has revealed. For now, we know who we can rely upon. Be appreciative for those who have stood beside you against the odds. They are the ones who won the battles. And finally, we should be spirit-filled and stand ready to fight. There will be other battles. Stand your ground.

ABOUT THE AUTHOR

Robert Null and his wife, Teri, have been engaged in full-time pastoral ministry for thirty-nine years. The last twenty-five of those years, they have served as senior pastors of First Assembly Meridian (FAM). In addition, Robert has served as presbyter and as an executive presbyter in the Mississippi District of the Assemblies of God. Robert and Teri have three daughters with families of their own who all attend church at FAM. Robert completed his undergraduate degree as Southwestern Assemblies of God College, now known as Southwestern University in Waxahachie, Texas. Robert completed his master's degree at Mississippi State University. Robert is a pastor, counselor, builder, part-time farmer, and a full-time granddad with seven grandchildren.

9 798886 443875